HOW TO BE HAPPY

Simple ways to build your confidence and resilience to become a happier, healthier you

Liggy Webb

CAPSTONE

This edition first published 2012

© 2012 Liggy Webb

Registered office

Capstone Publishing Ltd. (A Wiley Company), John Wiley and Sons Ltd, The Atrium, Southern Gate, Chichester, West Sussex, PO19 8SQ, United Kingdom

For details of our global editorial offices, for customer services and for information about how to apply for permission to reuse the copyright material in this book please see our website at www.wiley.com.

Peterborough City Council	
60000 0001 06046	
Askews & Holts	Jul-2013
158	£10.99

Library of Congress Cataloging-in-Publication Data is available

A catalogue record for this book is available from the British Library.

ISBN 978-0-857-08342-5 (paperback) ISBN 978-0-857-08339-5 (ebk)

ISBN 978-0-857-08340-1 (ebk) ISBN 978-0-857-08341-8 (ebk)

Set in 11 on 14 pt Myriad Pro by Toppan Best-set Premedia Limited

Printed in Great Britain by TJ International Ltd, Padstow, Cornwall, UK

This book is dedicated to my Mum and Dad, Robin and Ann.

You are my inspiration x

CONTENTS

PREFACE

I am a happiness explorer. I am captivated by the concept of happiness.

Having spent so much of my life researching, writing, presenting and speaking about this somewhat nebulous subject, I have deduced the following:

- Happiness is not out there!

- Happiness is a journey not a destination.

- Happiness is about taking personal responsibility.

Let me explain in a little more depth.

First of all I would like to address the plethora of consumerist activity that professes to deliver the silver bullet solution with regards to an individual's pursuit of happiness. It is frequently suggested that some purchase or material gain will make you happy, thereby reinforcing a belief that happiness is 'out there' somewhere. Many people waste valuable time looking in all the wrong places for something that they have been in possession of all along. The ability to be happy is inside everyone, we all have the capacity and it is completely free, no cost attached. You can make the decision to be happier right now if you really want to be.

Secondly, I don't believe that we have the ability to exist in a permanent state of happiness. To have a real zest for life – and feel passion and compassion – it is important to experience the full range of emotions that make up the rich tapestry of our lives. Life is a journey and so is happiness; as with many journeys, you may hit a few potholes along the way. Sometimes you may get hurt and feel pain. However, without experiencing any pain in your life you will be less likely to fully understand and appreciate happiness.

Finally, you need to take some personal responsibility for your own happiness. Often, people choose to play the victim and look to blame others for the way that they feel. They wallow and indulge themselves in constant pity parties, dragging others down at the same time by spreading their negative attitude germs.

The expectation that someone or something else will come along and make you happy is unrealistic. A key consideration with regards to happiness is the distance between reality and expectation. If you are constantly in a state of expectation, then you will constantly set yourself up for disappointment. If you are dependent on others to make you happy you may leave yourself vulnerable. It is essential to take personal responsibility.

Every person is unique and, by definition, what happiness means to one person will mean something different to another. You need to listen to yourself, define your own agenda and not allow anyone else to superimpose their version of happiness, otherwise you may lose control of what works for you. You need to be your own puppeteer and pull your own strings! So, the relationship you have with yourself is key. Being happy with who you are, what you do and what you have is not only advisable – I would say it is essential.

Happiness also takes practice. There may well be times in your life where there is simply too much darkness, times when the concept of happiness seems as far away as the moon. These are the times that you need to remind yourself about the things that make you feel happy and count your blessings one by one, over and over.

Creating a personal happiness toolkit will help you to feel more self-empowered and more in control. It will protect you from the inevitable media invasion of misery, and the negative 'doom goblins' that you sometimes meet along the way. It will also enable you to be more resilient and bounce back, quicker, better and stronger.

There are certainly a few things in my life that have given me a great education with regards to understanding happiness and what works in terms of developing a personal toolkit.

First of all, and perhaps the most insightful experience for me, has been a lifetime of managing bouts of depression. What I have learnt firsthand has been immense and drives me to want to explore how depression can be positively managed and how the stigma that is still attached to mental health issues can be addressed and dealt with. I have a great deal of empathy for people who don't experience depression and live or work with someone who does get depressed. The very nature of this insidious and seemingly invisible illness has far-reaching consequences for everyone.

Another great learning opportunity for me has been the work that I do with the United Nations – as an international consultant, travelling to various peace missions and duty stations around the world. Two of the most poignant experiences have been my trips to Afghanistan and Ethiopia, which I will tell you more about later in the book. It has most certainly brought a wider perspective to my world and a deeper understanding of what makes different people happy.

Certainly it challenges the Western approach to life. My belief is that if we spend as much time feeding our souls as we do attempting to feed our bank accounts we will be rewarded by a much healthier and more balanced perspective. We are likely to value things far more than we do and, in fact, derive more pleasure from what we have already, rather than constantly focusing on what we are missing or what other people have!

There are now an increasing number of organizations and movements that are championing the way forward for helping people to feel better about themselves and their lives. The aim of many of these is to understand happiness on a more wholesome level.

So, the aim of this book is to help you to feel better about yourself and your life. I certainly would not profess to say that by reading this book you will become instantly happy! It is up to you to use the information to work out your own happiness agenda. Life is what you make it.

I have endeavoured to keep the messages simple, and to demystify some of the complexities of modern living. I have started each chapter with an amusing story which I hope will bring a smile to your face. I have shared personal experiences, the wisdom of others and lots of useful tips and advice. You may already know something about most of the content that I have covered. But remember, it is not what you know, it is what you do with it that really counts.

Happy reading!

Liggy Webb

ACKNOWLEDGEMENTS

There are so many very special people in my life who have been instrumental in helping me to make this book happen. I am especially grateful to the following people. There is a little bit of each of you in this book.

Sara Pankhurst, Andy Veitch, Lawrence Mcilhoney, Jacky Leonard, Melanie Lisney, Jacky Pearson, Charles Christie-Webb, Lois Grant, Gary Lazarus, Fran Sherrington, Paula Evans, Andrew Sherrington, Isobel Sherrington, Aubrey Stuart, Kate Tuck, Paul O'Neill, Colin Botherston, Peter Stone, Hamish Mcleod, Andrew Gissing, Piera Cescutti, Colin Gautrey, Simon Reichwald, Chris Deakin, Sarah-Elizabeth Hall, Penny Foley, Maeve Price, Mary Earle, Yvonne Baxter, Caroline Schofield, Lynne Martinez, Mark Griffiths, Jane Hooper, Stephen Pauley, David Apparicio, Jo Apparicio, Richard Denny, Ciaran Beary and Brian Chaplain.

To my family, everyone who is part of The Learning Architect and to all the exceptionally talented writers who have yet to be discovered and belong to The Montpellier Writers Group.

I would also like to thank Jonathan Shipley for finding me and Grace O'Byrne, Vicky Kinsman, Emily Bryczkowski, Megan Saker, Jenny Ng, Louise Campbell, Laura Cooksley and everyone at Capstone who have been such a huge part of making this book happen.

Finally I would like to thank Nicholas Anderson for sharing the journey and making it such a fun and happy one.

AN
INTRODUCTION
TO HAPPINESS

*O*ne *day a man was sitting alone on a beach feeling reflective and melancholic. He looked out towards the sea as if searching for something. Suddenly he had an overwhelming urge to dive into the ocean to see if he could find whatever it was that was missing from his life.*

Just as he was about to run into the sea he was astonished to see a tiny mermaid, no larger than his hand, perched on a rock looking at him curiously.

Mesmerized, he moved closer towards her and, as he approached, she spoke to him saying, 'I have been watching you for quite some time. You seem to be looking for something. Can I help you?'

The man replied 'I have so many things in my life, but I feel as if there is something missing. Can you give it to me?'

To which the mermaid replied happily, 'Yes I have unlimited magical powers so I can give you anything you want.'

The man stared hopefully into the tiny mermaid's eyes and said, 'I want to feel happy'.

'All right', nodded the mermaid, and proceeded to take away everything the man possessed. She took away every talent he had, she damaged his health, she burnt down his home, she emptied his bank account and turned his family and friends into statues. Then, she threw herself back into the ocean and swam happily away.

A month later, as the man lay on the beach – bereft, lonely, hungry and struggling for survival – the mermaid returned and gave back to him everything that he had once possessed.

Two weeks later, the mermaid was swimming close to the shore. She saw the man on the beach enjoying a BBQ with his family and friends.

He looked so happy and, as she watched him, she noticed a smile of pure contentment on his face.

At last he had found what he was looking for.

****

This story highlights the importance of appreciating what you have, and how a constant undefined search can divert us from living with and loving what we have.

There are many things in life that influence happiness. In recent years there have been substantial developments in the science of well-being, with new evidence of the factors that affect happiness and how it can be measured. There is now the opportunity to use this evidence to make better choices about the way we live our lives, both at home and at work.

Health is an important consideration. In 1948, the World Health Organization defined the word 'health' as meaning 'physical, mental and social well-being, not merely the absence of disease or infirmity.'

In the light of this, we have the opportunity to embrace these key elements, to cultivate them and weave them into the rich tapestry of our lives.

SO WHAT IS HAPPINESS?

Happiness is currently front-page news. Recently, two Nobel Prize-winning economists, Joseph Stiglitz and Amartya Sen, called on world leaders to move away from a purely economic measure of value towards a broader vision that includes well-being and its sustainability.

Cash-strapped governments are investigating 'emotional well-being' (EWB) with the idea that an improvement in each nation's EWB could be a valuable asset, with a solid return on investment. Indeed, there is persuasive evidence that happier people make a greater contribution to society while making fewer demands on it.

For most of us, happiness is that pleasant feeling we get when life is good. It encompasses a wide range of feelings – from contentment to immense joy and elation – depending on how far up and down the emotional palette we each have the capacity to extend. But we all know it when we see it, and we like it. It is the ultimate feel-good factor.

We are taught from a very early age to seek happiness. As children our concept of happiness is quite simple but, as the years pass, this becomes greatly expanded. We come to believe that if we succeed at something, whether it is a career or a relationship, we will be happy. Some people seek out happiness through religion or a spiritual leader and, it seems, everyone has their own idea as to what makes them happy. The searching often becomes the very point of our existence. If someone asks us what we want, for ourselves or our loved ones, the likely response is 'happiness'.

What constitutes happiness or, perhaps more pertinently, where happiness exists are questions that have troubled many a great thinker.

The philosopher, Aristotle, believed that happiness was the meaning and the purpose of life, the whole aim and object of human existence. He believed that we choose happiness always for itself, and never for the sake of something else. It is the end to which all virtuous actions are directed. It must be some good or set of goods that, in themselves, make life worth living.

SOME OF THE SCIENCE BEHIND HAPPINESS

Many people chase happiness by acquiring material goods. However, scientific studies support the age-old saying that 'money doesn't buy happiness'.

Psychologist Tal Ben-Shahar defines happiness as 'the overall experience of pleasure and meaning'. He describes it as the ultimate currency, the end to which all other ends lead, and the indicator by which we measure our lives.

Psychologist Martin Seligman, Director of the Positive Psychology Center at the University of Pennsylvania and founder of positive psychology (a branch of psychology which focuses on the empirical study of such things as positive emotions, strengths-based character, and healthy institutions), defines a formula for happiness:

$H = S + C + V$

- S is your happiness set point

- C constitutes your life circumstances

- V represents your voluntary activities.

S, a combination of genetic disposition and cultural upbringing, is largely out of your control. C, your life circumstances, may also be difficult to change. But V is where you have total control and opportunity. The activities in which you engage and the way you choose to think about your life offer you the opportunity for greater happiness. Positive psychology is essentially about what makes life worth living.

Other psychologists also suggest that happiness is not a destination, but a process. Rather than viewing life as a period of necessary hardship and struggle with the promise of happiness at retirement or beyond, you can reasonably strive to find happiness every day.

Tal Ben-Shahar suggests that rather than ask yourself if you're happy, a better question might be: 'How can I become happier?' This suggests that there is always the possibility for greater positive feelings, and urges you to reach continually for a sense of well-being in order to attract the good things in life.

WHOLESOME HAPPINESS

I love the word 'wholesome', especially when it is attributed to happiness. It focuses on a more balanced and sustainable approach rather than the quick-fix hedonism that modern society seems not only to condone but to encourage and celebrate.

The consideration of the mind, body and soul working in harmony seems a very sensible approach, especially when the term 'work–life balance' is used so frequently in business as a solution to the ever-increasing stress-related illnesses that have such a negative impact on the economy.

Balance is key, as is understanding our core values.

I was exploring the concept of wholesome happiness and personal values a while ago whilst I was in Afghanistan doing some work with the UN.

I was especially curious and excited about visiting Kabul. Watching the news and hearing so many stories had filled me with some trepidation. What I found, however, despite the underlying tension, the obvious poverty, the guns, the guards and the grime, was the raw beauty of the country and, most of all, the people.

One conversation that resonated with me most of all was when I was speaking with one of the delegates in my group. He was a mullah – a Muslim man educated in Islamic theology and sacred law. He had been working with the United Nations Office on Drugs and Crime for some years. I shared with him some of my research and we discussed at length the concept of happiness and the appreciation of life.

As you can imagine, the situation and circumstances in Afghanistan are incredibly challenging and, from a Western perspective, it can be difficult to comprehend what people would have to be grateful for, or happy about.

However, as I shared this somewhat narrow view, I was immediately challenged by the mullah, who looked at me with calm and gentle eyes and said: 'Being happy in life isn't so complicated. I have come to appreciate that as long as you have something to love, something to do that gives you a purpose and something to hope for and believe in, then you will always have something to be happy about and grateful for.'

HOW TO BE HAPPIER

The challenges that face us in modern life, such as finding purpose, defining ourselves and managing stress, are numerous and complex. There is so much pressure to prove ourselves, so many unrealistic role models that we are encouraged to emulate. The pace of life is overwhelming; we don't have time to do the things we really want to. Parents don't spend enough quality time with their children. People feel more isolated, more neglected and everyone is playing catch up. Our thinking ability, relationship with others and the relationship we have with ourselves is in jeopardy.

Every person is entitled to feel down at times but we need to develop a set of skills to help ourselves to be happier if we really want to get the best and most out of life. We don't need to settle for mediocre when the quality of our existence can be so much more fulfilling and meaningful.

Over the next twelve chapters I have addressed some of the key components to help you to be happier.

Taking personal responsibility and making the best of who you are with regards to your attitude and your health will lay a very positive foundation. Coping with stress, managing change and having the ability to bounce back quickly will develop your personal resilience and emotional strength.

Being open to learning new things, encouraging and sustaining positive relationships and getting your work–life balance into a healthy perspective will help you to flourish. Developing an attitude of gratitude will help you to appreciate your life more. Learning how to be kinder and more compassionate, and knowing that you can make a difference, will truly inspire you to live a more meaningful life.

Happiness is contagious and, if we work on making ourselves happier, we will be in a far better position to help others to be happier too.

Happiness resides not in possessions and not in gold. The feeling of happiness dwells in the soul.

Democritus

1

LIFE IS WHAT YOU MAKE IT

For there is nothing good or bad, but thinking makes it so

William Shakespeare

A little boy called Andy was asked to audition with his classmates for a part in the school play. His mother knew that Andy had his heart set on being in the play and she feared how he would react if he was not chosen.

On the day that the parts were awarded, Andy's mother went to the school to collect him feeling anxious about the outcome.

Seeing his mother, Andy rushed up to her, eyes shining with pride and excitement. 'Guess what Mum', he shouted. Then, with words that can provide a lesson to us all, he said, 'I've been chosen to clap and cheer.'

****

I remember, when I was about ten, I had a little purple autograph book. I asked a friend of my sister to write in it and she inscribed the words: 'Life is what YOU make it!' Those words stuck in my mind and have become a personal mantra, even through some of the most difficult and painful times.

Understanding and knowing that we are more in control of our lives than we sometimes believe is not only reassuring, it is empowering. The way that we think determines the way that we feel and is the control pad for the volume of happiness that we choose to experience in our lives. The quality of thinking essentially determines the quality of life.

Your perspective is your reality and your reality is your perspective. We can make a conscious choice about how we want to interpret every situation. It's the glass half-empty or half-full approach. It's the little boy who celebrates and gets excited about the opportunity to clap and cheer.

THE POWER OF POSITIVE THINKING

I certainly know from first-hand experience that a firm belief in the power of positive thinking has bailed me out of many potentially derailing situations.

Thinking positively is not about putting your head in the sand, nor is it about being unrealistic. By developing a positive attitude you still recognize the negative aspects of a situation. However, you choose to focus on the hope and opportunity that is available. This approach helps you to avoid getting locked into a paralyzing loop of bad feeling, and allows you to move on quickly, take action to solve problems and embrace challenges in life that we inevitably experience.

Pressure and stress-related illness are increasingly features of modern-day living. We are all human, and we are designed to experience the whole palette of emotions. Fear and anxiety can grip us all. It is how we manage these challenging situations that is a prerequisite for our overall well-being in the long term.

The writings and teachings of some of the great philosophers over the last 2000 years have been significant. From Epictetus, who said 'What concerns me is not the way things are, but rather the way people think things are', to my favourite quote by Shakespeare who so keenly observed: 'There is nothing either good or bad, but thinking makes it so'.

The viewpoint extends over centuries from Norman Vincent Peale and his emphasis on the power of positive thinking, to the American psychotherapist Albert Ellis, the creator of rational emotive behavioural therapy (REBT), which led to the formulation of cognitive behavioural therapy (CBT) – something you may have come across already and something I applaud.

With so many people now rushing to the doctors for a quick-fix subscription of 'happy pills', CBT can be a very potent alternative.

The word 'cognitive' is a term to describe thinking, and the word 'behavioural' is there to emphasize that change is not just about how we think, but also about what we actually do with that thinking.

One of the premier psychologists of our day, Martin Seligman, having first gained prominence in researching depression began to look at factors that contribute to positive emotional health. Seligman and his colleagues identified 24 key factors associated with individuals who report high levels of life satisfaction. The most recent research suggests that out of these 24, five are particularly important: optimism, zest for life, curiosity, the ability to love and be loved, and gratitude.

So, certainly, by being optimistic and by being hopeful of positive outcomes is a step in the right direction.

> *Whether you are an optimist or a pessimist might not affect the outcome, it's just that the optimist has a better time in life!*
>
> **James Borg, *Mind Power***

WHAT IS A POSITIVE MENTAL ATTITUDE?

The term 'positive mental attitude' (PMA) has almost become a bit of a cliché. Many books on success or self-improvement start with a sharp focus on cultivating energy, enthusiasm and optimism in all areas of your life and, in my view, quite rightly so. Developing a positive attitude is the key to health and happiness.

Positivity and optimism are now known to be a root cause of many life benefits. The relatively new science of psychoneuroimmunology looks at how the mind can influence the immune system. The theory is that you will live longer, and be healthier and happier, by cultivating a positive attitude towards life. In addition, you're more likely to be successful, maintain better relationships and have a beneficial influence on those around you.

THINK ABOUT YOUR THOUGHTS

Identifying and analyzing your thoughts, and understanding your beliefs, are the key to dealing with your life positively.

Did you know we have, on average, about 60–80,000 thoughts a day and the quality of those thoughts is responsible for how we feel and behave? Here is a little poem I have written that will give you something to ponder on.

Yesterday I had a thought.

That thought became an emotion

That emotion turned into words, the words fuelled action,

The actions became a habit. My habits are my Character,

My Character defines my destiny.

Today, therefore,

I'll think about my thoughts a little more.

YOU AND YOUR EMOTIONS

One of the most basic indicators of positivity or negativity is the type and range of emotions that you experience. Emotions can have a very strong impact on how you behave and react. One fascinating idea that is well worth reading about, and which can help you to become more emotionally aware, is that of emotional intelligence. The essential premise of emotional intelligence is that, in order to be successful, interpersonally and intrapersonally, you need awareness, control and management of your own emotions in order to recognize and understand the emotions of those around you.

It is important also to be aware that you feed your emotions with your thoughts.

Imagine you are hosting a dinner party for all your emotions and they are sitting around the dinner table hungrily waiting to be fed. All the usual suspects are there like fear, anger, jealousy, happiness, optimism, joy and an assortment of the good, the bad and the downright ugly. You are there as the host of the dinner party and you can choose which emotion you want to feed.

In the same way, by choosing what you think, you can starve the negative emotions and feed up and boost the health of the positive ones. You are in fact the nutritionist of your soul. What a great concept!

It also helps to remember that, at the bedrock of your thoughts and emotions, are your values and beliefs – deep-rooted ideas that are a result of all your life experiences. These are your life attitudes and they colour and shape your perception of the world. Whereas thoughts are relative, beliefs tend to feel completely true, undeniable and resolute. Negative beliefs, however, can undermine your

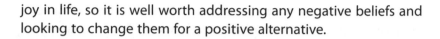

joy in life, so it is well worth addressing any negative beliefs and looking to change them for a positive alternative.

Being consciously aware of your thoughts, feelings and beliefs can be a very useful exercise and the ability to challenge our thoughts can be a positive step in helping us to identify negative behaviours and, ultimately, discover positive solutions to problems and opportunities.

I was delighted to find that a new word has been introduced into our vocabulary called 'probortunity'. This inclusive word combines the word problem and opportunity to describe something you want to improve and change for the better. When faced with any problem at home or in the workplace try replacing the word problem with opportunity and, rather than focus on the negatives, actively seek out all the solutions and possibilities. Become a possibilitarian!

UNDERSTANDING HABITS

It is also important to be aware that about 90 per cent of what we think and do is habitual, which means that many of our day-to-day routines are something that we just do and don't necessarily think about on a conscious level. To change any of our behaviours we need to address our thinking and redefine our habits. This can take quite a bit of effort and sometimes we can fall at the first hurdle and give up. In a world that is geared towards instant gratification it may be easier to seek a more immediate solution. My personal view is that if something is worth it, and we stick at it and achieve it for ourselves, the reward is far more pleasurable. Positive thinking and positive self talk is a habit anyone can adopt with some practice, irrespective of their background, education and experience.

The human brain is a magnificent machine and consists of billions of nerve cells with innumerable extensions. This interlacing of nerve fibres and their junctions allows a nerve impulse to follow a number of routes known as neural pathways. When you learn something new, your brain makes connections that create new pathways for activity. Setting up neural pathways is actually quite simple. If a newly learned behaviour is repeated enough times, it eventually gets programmed into the subconscious mind; that behaviour becomes automatic and we no longer have to think about doing it, because we respond automatically. This, simply put, is a habit.

Have you ever arrived at home or work with no memory of how you got there? When you started on your journey, you thought about the first few steps on that familiar path, but somewhere along the way, your brain moved onto more interesting topics, and the next thing you knew, you'd arrived. This is the essence of habits: once you start on a familiar series of actions, you stop thinking about them and you are able to complete them without conscious thought or attention.

Cache memory in a computer is another good analogy. The computer stores commonly used actions where it can access and process them faster. The brain does the same thing. This can work in both a positive and negative way: it can free our minds from dull or repetitive tasks, but it also makes it difficult to stop once we've started.

What separates the positive and negative people is that the positive people have habits and behaviours that are conducive to success, while the negative people have ones that facilitate failure in their lives. Remember: you control your habits – they do not control you. Your life is the culmination of all the daily behaviours that you have.

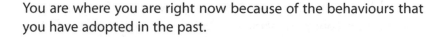

You are where you are right now because of the behaviours that you have adopted in the past.

It is important to identify which habits in your life lead to negative consequences and which lead to positive rewards. The difficulty in this sometimes has to do with instant gratification. If you change your habits then, more often than not, you're not going to see an immediate effect. It is for this reason that people struggle with diets or can't stop drinking, smoking, or spending money because they can't control the instant gratification that is delivered.

Experts in hypnosis and neuro-linguistic programming (NLP – the art and science of personal excellence) believe that it takes around 21 to 28 days to form the basis of a new habit or behaviour. The time it takes to replace an old one is inconclusive because it depends entirely on the person and how long they have owned it.

Think of behaviour as a tree. A young tree has short roots that you can pull straight from the ground. A behaviour that you have owned for many years is like an adult tree that has long roots that extend far underground.

Human beings tend to take actions to either move them closer to pleasure or away from pain. With that in mind, analyze your bad habits and dig down for the factors underlying them. Why do you eat so much? Why do you drink so much? Why are you negative? Behind all of these habits and behaviours lies a reason. Changing a bad behaviour without addressing the root cause of the problem will only lead to a regression.

As with any newly learned behaviour, you may well experience some internal resistance for the first week or more. This is natural and it's not going to be easy, so you have to mentally prepare for this challenge ahead of time. After you survive this first week, you will find that your new habit and behaviour becomes easier and easier to do, and soon you don't even have to think about doing it at all.

Stress is the primary cause of people reverting back to their old patterns of behaviour, so be wary of the level of stress in your life and know that a high amount can wipe away a new habit and make you revert back to your old ones.

SUSTAINING A POSITIVE ATTITUDE

Creating and maintaining a positive attitude is the most efficient and low-cost investment you can make in order to improve your life. As I have explained, a positive way of thinking is a habit that must be learned through repetition and conscious effort on your part.

Positive affirmations to condition your mind can be very useful. Try saying things to yourself like: 'I am an optimistic, hopeful, positive thinking person. Yes I accept that bad things can happen in my life, however I choose to look for positive opportunities and out-comes in every situation.'

The question I ask myself every time I encounter a perceived problem is 'what is the probortunity?' It can make a big difference whether you see darkness through the light or whether you choose to see brightness through the shadows.

A positive attitude is not dependent upon your genetic composi-tion: even if you are predisposed to negative thinking you can learn to move your thinking to the positive side.

This depends entirely upon you and how you choose to think.

AVOID NEGATIVE ATTITUDE GERMS

I have been lucky enough to meet, and work with, some highly successful and inspiring people. What sets them apart and makes them special is their ability to turn a potentially negative thought into a positive one. They are also acutely aware of their attitude and how it affects others around them. They take responsibility for their NAGs – negative attitude germs!

Let me ask you a question. If you had a really bad cold or flu would you walk over to someone and sneeze in their face? Hopefully not!

So let me ask you another question. Have you ever had a bad day when someone or something has annoyed or upset you and you have felt the need to get it off your chest and tell someone else all about it? I am sure that we have all been guilty of that from time to time.

You are, in effect, spreading your NAGs – negative attitude germs.

You may have noticed that when you are with someone who is suffering from a physical or emotional problem, you feel bad too. It's often described as catching their emotion. Researchers have observed this actually happening in real time in the brain, using an advanced magnetic resonance imaging (MRI) machine. It shows the brain of Person A reflects activity in the same area as Person B when they are in close proximity.

The scientific term for this is 'neural mirroring'. This graphically illustrates the danger of hanging around negative, pessimistic people if you prefer to be positive and optimistic. You can 'catch' their NAGs just by being in close proximity.

BE A RADIATOR

Some people you meet are like drains: negative, listless, doom goblins; and when we come into contact with them they drain us of energy. They like to tell you about all their negative news and prefer to play the victim, wallowing in the 'poor me' mentality. These are the people who when you ask them how they are they will respond with their shoulders slumped, eyelids drooped 'Well you know ... I feel really ... bad!' and then they will give you a graphic blow-by-blow account of all their woes and feelings of impending doom! You may well know people like this. Perhaps it is a behaviour you indulge in? Perhaps we all do from time to time, but does it really do us any favours?

Other people, however, are like radiators – full of warmth and vitality. We feel positively energized by them. They appear bright and radiant, look you in the eye and, when you ask them how they are, they smile and tell you something positive.

It is amazing how some are so intent on being negative. I wonder whether they get up some days and plan to go into work to 'drain the radiators'! You may well know people like this. It might even be a behaviour that you indulge in. If so, next time you find yourself doing this ask yourself how you will positively benefit from choosing this mindset.

TAKE PERSONAL RESPONSIBILITY

The antidote for negativity is that you accept complete responsibility for your situation. The very act of taking responsibility short-circuits and cancels out any negative emotion that you may trigger. By embracing responsibility you will reap many rewards. The successes brought by this attitude act as a foundation for self-respect, pride and confidence. Responsibility breeds competence and power. By living up to our promises and obligations, we win the trust of others. Once we are seen as trustworthy, people will willingly work with us for our mutual gain. Making excuses can put the brakes on our progress, while accepting responsibility can lead us to succeed.

It is easy to blame others or circumstances for everything in our lives – past, present and future. It lets us off the hook to some degree. However, ultimately it doesn't help us because we become a prisoner of circumstance and allow everything and everyone around us to dictate our world.

The workplace very often can breed a 'blame culture' where everyone is looking for someone else to blame when things go wrong. Taking personal responsibility is a challenge for some people. Perhaps it is a fear of admitting mistakes which can be perceived by some as failing. However, making mistakes is human and we can't get everything right all the time. To increase your rate of success you will have to be willing to accept that you will make mistakes along the way, the skill is to positively learn from them. Certainly some of the best learning and character-building experiences I have been through are on the back of big mistakes. As James Joyce so eloquently put it, 'Mistakes are the portals of discovery'.

Putting your hand in the air and saying 'yes I recognize I made a mistake', or 'I am responsible for that and this is what I am going to do to improve the situation' is actually quite liberating. Try it.

For example, admitting when we get something wrong and saying 'I'm sorry' can relieve a great deal of tension in any relationship. Humble pie can actually taste quite nice, and it certainly isn't poisonous. I have a huge amount of respect for people who are brave enough to admit when they don't get something right and have the humility to accept it, acknowledge it and then positively move on.

Just because we admit mistakes it doesn't make us a lesser person or inferior to others.

No one can make you feel inferior without your consent.

Eleanor Roosevelt

Have you ever heard yourself in an argument say 'This is how YOU made me feel'? The truth of the matter is that no one can actually make you feel anything if you don't allow them to. You choose how you respond and ultimately feel.

Life is a journey and, granted, you may get a little travel sick along the way and you may hit a few potholes. However, by developing a positive attitude you will be much better equipped for dealing with setbacks. It takes practice and, for sure, there will be days when you really struggle to see the sun through the clouds. You may well decide you want to wallow a little and that is OK. The question though is, for how long?

Life is what you make it and what makes your life worth living is your own personal quest and adventure. How exciting and wonderful is that?

Life is what you make it: top tips

✓ The first step to happiness is to make a conscious decision to be happy
✓ Choose to be an optimist not a pessimist
✓ Use the word probortunity and actively seek out opportunities

✓ Think more consciously about what you think about
✓ Address any negative attitude germs that you may be spreading
✓ Choose to be a radiator not a drain
✓ Avoid blaming other people
✓ Learn from your mistakes and positively move on
✓ Take personal responsibility for all your actions
✓ Remember, this is your life and your life is what you make it

When I was five years old, my mother always told me that happiness was the key to life. When I went to school, they asked me what I wanted to be when I grew up. I wrote down 'happy'. They told me I didn't understand the assignment, and I told them they didn't understand life.

John Lennon

2

BE THE BEST
YOU CAN BE

When you feel good about yourself, others will feel good about you, too

Jake Steinfeld

A group of tiny frogs were holding a competition. The goal was to reach the top of a very high tower. A large crowd gathered around the tower to watch and cheer on the contestants.

The race began. When the frogs in the crowd looked at the height of the tower they didn't believe that any of the tiny frogs would reach the top.

One observer shouted out 'Oh that is far too difficult!' Another shouted 'They will never make it to the top!' The tiny frogs began to collapse. One by one they fell down the tower, except for those who in a fresh tempo kept climbing higher and higher.

The crowd continued to shout at them. 'It is too difficult! None of you will make it!' and, sure enough, more of the frogs gave up. However one tiny frog continued higher and higher and higher. This one wouldn't give up!

At the end of the competition, everyone else had given up climbing the tower, except for the one tiny frog who, after a big effort, was the only one who reached the top. All of the other tiny frogs naturally wanted to know how this one frog had managed to do it.

The winner, they discovered, was deaf.

****

Fear of failure is one of life's greatest limitations and can hold you back from achieving so much. We are essentially motivated and driven by two great emotions: fear and desire.

Many people choose to focus on fear. They impose self-limitations and don't achieve a fraction of what they are capable of because

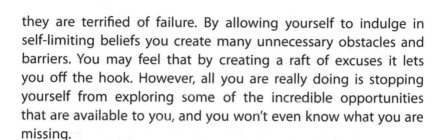

they are terrified of failure. By allowing yourself to indulge in self-limiting beliefs you create many unnecessary obstacles and barriers. You may feel that by creating a raft of excuses it lets you off the hook. However, all you are really doing is stopping yourself from exploring some of the incredible opportunities that are available to you, and you won't even know what you are missing.

If you want to be more successful you will need to take some risks and, rather than view outcomes as failure, view them as learning opportunities that help you grow. The acorn has the ability to grow into an oak tree and you have the opportunity, every single day of your life, to spread the branches within your mind and explore how to be the best you can be. You have to believe to achieve and not let other people, or the doubting fearful voice in your head, put you off.

ARE YOU YOUR OWN BEST FRIEND?

The most important relationship that you will ever have is the relationship you have with yourself. Would you choose to be your best friend? If you don't like yourself or believe in yourself then how do you expect anyone else to?

Take a good look at yourself in the metaphorical mirror and start by being really honest. What is your true opinion of yourself? Are you appreciative of all your strengths and qualities? Or do you beat yourself up on a regular basis about your misgivings, mistakes and weaknesses?

If it is the latter, I am sure that you would not consciously treat anyone else, let alone your best friend, that way. So why do we do it to ourselves? Why are we sometimes our own worst enemy?

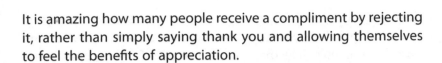

It is amazing how many people receive a compliment by rejecting it, rather than simply saying thank you and allowing themselves to feel the benefits of appreciation.

Lack of self-appreciation is one of the reasons people become depressed. Appreciating yourself is the most important component of self-love. However that sounds, it is hugely important because, if we don't love ourselves, how can we begin to expect anyone else to? People who appreciate themselves usually have a good heart and are full of optimism. They love and appreciate the gifts that they have bestowed upon them. They feel comfortable in themselves and are known for their generosity and tolerance.

We have to take responsibility for being the best that we can be. So often we will compare ourselves to others and, if we do this, we run the danger of engendering one of two emotions – vanity or bitterness – because there will always be people we perceive as better or worse off than ourselves. It can be fruitless to benchmark ourselves against others. Using yourself as your own benchmark is far more constructive.

So, the first step to achieving your personal best is to be your own best friend. Take time to have a little chat with yourself, and really listen and observe the way you treat yourself. Be kinder, be more considerate, be more positive.

SELF-AWARENESS

Self-awareness is a recognition of our personality, our strengths and weaknesses, our likes and dislikes. Knowing and understanding who you are and what makes you tick is essential if you want to unveil your inner happiness. Developing self-awareness can help you to recognize when you are stressed or under pressure. It

is a prerequisite for effective communication and interpersonal relations, and essential for developing empathy for others.

Self-awareness is the first step in the creation process. As you grow in self-awareness, you will understand better why you feel what you feel and behave as you behave. That understanding then gives you the opportunity and freedom to change those things you'd like to change about yourself and create the life you want. Without fully knowing who you are, self-acceptance and change is impossible.

As you come to know yourself better, you will begin to shed your inhibitions. In enhancing your self-awareness, you will have the confidence to be more open, to share relevant information, to improve communication and connect better with others.

One tool to help you with this is the *Johari Window* – a model developed in 1955 and named after the first names of its inventors, Joseph Luft and Harrington Ingham. It is one of the most useful models for describing the process of human interaction. Based on a four-paned 'window', it divides personal awareness into four different types, as represented by its four quadrants: open, hidden, blind, and unknown.

Begin with the 'open' pane, which is your 'arena'. This is what you and other people know about you. The second 'closed' pane is your 'façade', which is what you know about yourself, but others do not. Essentially this is your secret space, representing the things you keep to yourself – either because you want to keep them private or you fear letting other people know about them in case they judge or reject you.

The third 'blind' pane is your 'blind spot' which is what others know about you, but you don't know about yourself. This could be something obvious like physical behaviours or mannerisms. The final 'unknown' pane is your personal potential. This is what you don't know about yourself, but neither does anybody else. It is your *unknown self*, waiting to be discovered; your potential, waiting to be unleashed.

So, in order to understand ourselves better and to feel the confidence to show ourselves more, we need to trust in order to be more open, and to be able to accept feedback so that we can learn more about ourselves from other perspectives.

Trust is something that requires a certain amount of confidence and also the ability to move out of our comfort zone on occasion. The ability to trust someone is a real gift. However, it is a gift that brings with it a certain vulnerability. Positive relationships are built on the cornerstone of trust. Sometimes it can be difficult to let go of the paranoia and fear that is the flipside of trust, especially if you have been let down or criticized. It may not be easy but, if you simply behave in the way that you would expect others to behave towards you, this will help you to build trust in yourself and others. It will help if you are honest with yourself and other people. There is much truth in the saying 'you reap what you sow', and you will attract honest, trustworthy people if you behave in an honest and trustworthy fashion.

Receiving feedback can also be challenging. It is the food of progress. However, like some foods, while it may be good for us, it can also be a little unpleasant to digest. However, the more you can let your guard down and open up, and the more you see feedback as free information that can add huge value, or be dissuaded (it is *your* choice after all), the more potential you have to grow and see yourself more clearly in the metaphorical mirror. In Chapter 8 I will focus on trust and feedback in more detail.

SELF-CONFIDENCE

Working on your self-confidence is a very good investment of time. There is a fine line between arrogance and confidence, and it is important to be honest with yourself, and also seek feedback from others to gain a balanced perspective. It is also important, however, that you don't rely on others to big you up and make you feel better. It is important that you learn how to recognize and appreciate yourself when you have done something well. If you rely on others or become so preoccupied with other peoples' opinions of you, it can create insecurity and paranoia.

Imagine having no one to compare yourself with except you. What a sense of relief this would bring. You wouldn't have to worry about not looking like the alpha male or female with the smartest mind, the most important job role and the biggest pay packet. You wouldn't have to worry about your body not being the youngest, most beautiful and most sexy.

All you would have to think is: did I do this activity better than I did it last week? Have I moved forward in my own definition of success? Am I feeling peaceful; doing my best for my health? Do I have an attractive mind and healthy interactions with other people?

Most people would never admit to making comparisons with other people – to do so implies jealousy and small-mindedness. However, everyone has undoubtedly taken a measure of themselves at some point by reference to someone else – even if only subconsciously.

Being the best that we can be is the most realistic ambition. We are essentially people in progress. I like this concept. It means that we can always improve, and as long as we head in the right direction with the right intention, then every breath we take is a breath worth taking.

The real key to self-confidence is about believing in yourself and trusting your own views and opinions. At times, this can be difficult, especially if you have a tendency to listen to others and benchmark yourself against what they think of you. However, this can be dangerous; the ability to establish your own inner benchmark to success is essential.

Every human being has the means to take control and make positive changes. Other people can try and stop you, but only if you let them. When you look in the mirror, be proud of the person that you see, knowing that you do the best you can. Tell yourself that you are confident and believe in yourself. Focus on your strengths and the positive aspects of your character, and set about developing the areas that you have for potential.

The way a person carries themselves tells a story. People with slumped shoulders and lethargic movements display a lack of self-confidence. They aren't enthusiastic about what they're doing and they don't consider themselves important. By practising good posture, you'll automatically feel more confident. Stand up straight, keep your head up, and make eye contact. You'll make a positive impression on others and instantly feel more alert and empowered.

BRING OUT THE BEST IN YOURSELF

When we think negatively about ourselves, we often project that feeling on to others in the form of insults and gossip. To break this cycle of negativity, get into the habit of praising other people.

Refuse to engage in backstabbing gossip and make an effort to compliment those around you instead. In the process, you'll become well-liked and, by looking for the best in others, you will, indirectly, bring out the best in yourself.

In meetings and public assemblies around the world, I have noticed that people constantly strive to sit at the back of the room. Most people prefer the back because they're afraid of being noticed. This reflects a lack of self-confidence. It begs the question: do you want to sit in the back row of life or the front?

I have also noticed that during group discussions and meetings in the workplace, many people never speak up because they're afraid that other people will judge them for saying something stupid. This fear isn't really justified. Generally, people are much more accepting than we imagine. In fact, most people are dealing with the exact same fears. By making an effort to speak up at least once in every group discussion, you'll become a better public speaker and more confident in your own thoughts and abilities. Pushing yourself out of your comfort zone sometimes is very good for you.

Along the same lines as personal appearance, physical fitness has a huge effect on self-confidence. If you're out of shape, you're likely to feel insecure, unattractive, and less energetic. By keeping fit, you improve your physical appearance, energize yourself, and accomplish something positive. Having the discipline to exercise not only makes you feel better; it creates positive momentum that you can build on for the rest of the day.

Too often we get caught up in our own desires. We focus too much on ourselves and not enough on the needs of other people. If you stop thinking about yourself and concentrate on the contribution you're making to the rest of the world, you won't worry as much about you own flaws. This will increase self-confidence and allow you to contribute with maximum efficiency. The more you contribute to the world, the more you'll be rewarded with personal success and recognition.

NEGATIVE INHIBITING THOUGHTS

Another term for negative inhibiting thoughts is 'excuses'. Lets' face it, we probably all use them. Some people become highly skilled at excuse making. It lets us off the hook and aids us in unleashing ourselves from the burden of responsibility. It also stops us from achieving some amazing things.Whatever your excuses are – whether it is because you are too old, too young, too busy, you don't have enough money, or it didn't work last time – stop right there and challenge yourself.

Excuses are harmful. These negative inhibiting thoughts prevent us from succeeding. When we make excuses, and repeat them often enough, they become a belief. This belief then becomes a self-fulfilling prophecy. Nothing is impossible in this world. Indeed, add a space to 'impossible' and it becomes 'I'm possible'. I often think the saddest thing we could ever say to ourselves when our time is up would be: 'If only'. It's much more likely that you will regret the things you didn't do rather than the ones you did. If you want to live a fulfilled and enriched life, sometimes you need to challenge your self-imposed boundaries.

As we observed at the beginning of the chapter, people are essentially driven by two things: fear and desire. If you are not careful, you might allow fear to stop you from trying new things, just in case you make a mistake. However, for every mistake that you make, another valuable lesson is learnt. So, on a very positive note, you are building your pot of wisdom.

POSITIVE SELF-TALK

It's time to have a little chat with yourself, and to check out your personal vocabulary. How do you talk to yourself? Vocabulary is something we very rarely pay conscious attention to, yet it can give away a whole host of information about us to the perceptive listener.

Your appearance, vocabulary and speech form part of that all-important first impression we make on other people. While the tone and timbre of our voice creates either a pleasing or grating effect on the listener, our choice of words conveys our attitude and emotional stance. There is a very interesting relationship between vocabulary and attitude.

When you describe an emotional state or use words to express an emotion directly, you reinforce that emotion. If, for example, you say, 'Damn!' when you make a mistake, you reinforce the anger you feel about the mistake. If instead however you say 'Oops!' you're conveying to your subconscious mind that the mistake was minor, something not worth getting too worked up about.

Modifying your vocabulary is one way to reduce the number of times you experience strong, stressful emotions like anger. The same principle applies to positive emotions.

Have you ever asked someone how they are and they answered, 'Not too bad, thanks'. What if they'd answered instead, 'I'm really good thank you', or 'I'm feeling great. Thanks for asking!' How would that affect the person's attitude towards his or her life?

Positive self-talk is a great way to improve your energy levels. Most people know this by the more straightforward name of affirmation. But you need something a bit more focused than the traditional: 'Every day in every way, I'm getting better and better'. When you are using positive self-talk to improve your energy levels you need to make sure that your subconscious is in no doubt as to what you are talking about.

When you are doing the affirmations, make sure that you have a very clear goal in mind as to what you are trying to achieve. If your wording is too vague, or you are not focused enough on what you are trying to achieve, then you may not get the results that you are looking for. For instance, if you are trying to encourage yourself to go for a good long walk every day, there is no point in making a vague statement to yourself such as 'I would like to get out and about more'.

You need to be very clear as to what you are trying to encourage yourself to do. A much more concise affirmation would be, 'I go for a walk every day in the park when I get back from work and it is very enjoyable'. This way the mind is left in no doubt as to what you are trying to achieve and what is required of it.

When you are making affirmations to improve your energy levels, it is very important that all of these affirmations are in the present tense, and are also in the positive. It is essential to keep the affirmations in the positive as the subconscious mind is not able to process a negative very well.

Rather than trying to get the subconscious mind to extract a positive action from a negative affirmation, it is much easier to put the affirmation in the positive in the first place. A good example of this would be for someone who is trying to lose weight using affirmations. If the affirmation is in the negative, for example, 'I will not eat fast food any more', then it is very difficult for the subconscious mind to process.

The mind not only has to process the negative, i.e. what you are *not* going to do – eat fast food – it also has to then decide subconsciously, what it is actually supposed to be doing instead. In this example, it would be 'eating well', but this in itself is not a clearly defined concept. On the other hand, if you put the affirmation in a positive sense, 'I am eating fresh fruit and salad every day' then it is very clear what is required of the mind and it is much easier to process this into action.

When you are doing positive self-talk, it is necessary to do it on a regular and consistent basis. The effects are usually cumulative and you should find that the more you do it, the more effective it is in helping you to build up your energy levels and to improve the way in which you live. This is partly due to the effect of saying something over and over again, but also, if your mind is used to you using affirmations and to processing them into action, then it is more likely to be able to process new affirmations as it is just following on in the pattern of the previous, albeit different, affirmations that you have used in the past. This way you can gain the benefits more quickly but you still need to use repetitions of the positive self-talk until you have achieved the right results.

MOTIVATIONAL SUPPORT

Personally, I find positive quotes and speeches very helpful and this extract from *A Return To Love: Reflections on the Principles of A Course in Miracles* by Marianne Williamson is so motivating and empowering for me. It epitomizes, quite perfectly, the need for us to embrace the potential within us confidently and positively:

> Our deepest fear is not that we are inadequate. Our deepest fear is that we are powerful beyond measure. It is our light, not our darkness that most frightens us. We ask ourselves, Who am I to be brilliant, gorgeous, talented, fabulous? Actually, who are you *not* to be? You are a child of God. Your playing small does not serve the world. There

is nothing enlightened about shrinking so that other people won't feel insecure around you. We are all meant to shine, as children do. We were born to make manifest the glory of God that is within us. It's not just in some of us; it's in everyone. And as we let our own light shine, we unconsciously give other people permission to do the same. As we are liberated from our own fear, our presence automatically liberates others.

I think this sums up quite beautifully the gift that we have been given, reminding us that we each have the permission to be the very best that we can be.

Be the best you can be: top tips

✓ Be your own best friend
✓ Have a little chat with yourself and listen to your inner dialogue
✓ Decide that you want to be the best that you can be
✓ Challenge your boundaries and step out of your comfort zone from time to time
✓ Be open and positive about change
✓ Be receptive to feedback, and learn to trust more
✓ Learn from your mistakes and grow
✓ Challenge your own limiting beliefs and excuses
✓ Avoid comparing yourself to others
✓ Develop your self-confidence and believe in yourself

Make the most of yourself, for that is all there is of you

Ralph Waldo Emerson

3

FIT FOR LIFE

The greatest wealth is health

Virgil

*M*r and Mrs Jones, an elderly couple who had been married for nearly 60 years, went on a very rare holiday. Although they were not very well off financially, they were in very good health This was due to the intervention of Mrs Jones who had insisted on a very strict diet of healthy foods, absolutely no refined carbohydrates, no alcohol, no smoking, and lots of exercise and morning yoga.

Sadly, on the way, their plane crashed and, as they both entered heaven, they were met at the entrance by an angel and escorted to a waiting limousine. Driving through beautiful countryside they drew up at a splendid mansion and were shown inside. It was furnished in gold and fine silks, had a sumptuous lounge, an indoor and outdoor Jacuzzi, plus a fully equipped kitchen stocked with an abundance of wonderful food and drink. They both gasped in astonishment when they were told, 'Welcome to heaven. This will be your home now.'

Mr Jones, who had learnt to be very frugal in his lifetime, immediately asked how much all of it was going to cost. 'Nothing', he was told 'this is heaven'.

Mr Jones looked out of the window and saw a magnificent championship golf course.

'What are the green fees?' he asked suspiciously.

'This is heaven', the angel replied, 'You can play for free whenever you wish'.

Next, they went to the clubhouse and saw the lavish buffet lunch, with every imaginable cuisine laid out before them.

Anticipating the old man's next question, the angel said, 'Don't ask, this is heaven, it is all free for you to enjoy'.

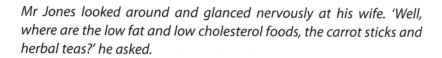

Mr Jones looked around and glanced nervously at his wife. 'Well, where are the low fat and low cholesterol foods, the carrot sticks and herbal teas?' he asked.

'This is heaven. You can eat and drink as much as you like, and you will never get overweight or sick', the angel reassured him.

'Do you mean that I don't need to do daily exercise or yoga anymore?' Mr Jones exclaimed.

'Not unless you want to', the angel said.

'No blood pressure test and annual medicals . . .'

'Never again. All you do here is just relax and indulge yourselves to your heart's content.'

Mr Jones sighed heavily and then glared at his wife and said 'You and your yoga and bran muffins. We could have been here ten years ago!'

****

It is becoming increasingly important to invest in our health. We are now living longer than we ever have done. In Western society we spend a great deal of time focusing on our pensions and savings. However, we don't always think about what the state of our health will be like when we finally retire.

I am not suggesting for one minute that you have to live the strict regime of poor old Mr Jones – and some people can take it a bit too far. However, a healthy balance is really important. Good health is about a blend of healthy eating and exercise. It's not about faddy diets and burn out at the gym. It's about being fit for life in a way that you are comfortable with. An investment in good health is a solid building block for happiness – because the better you feel physically, the better you will feel mentally and emotionally. A holistic approach to well-being is essential.

HEALTH IN THE 21ST CENTURY

According to the World Health Organisation, cardiovascular diseases are the leading cause of death in the world. These are diseases of the heart and blood vessels that can cause heart attacks and stroke. That is the bad news. The good news is that, in most cases, it is preventable. Apart from a few genetically inherited cases, there is nothing natural about dying from a heart attack.

Even more worrying is the fact that heart disease is occurring at a younger and younger age. Clearly something about our lifestyle, diet or even environment has changed radically in the last 60 years to bring on this modern epidemic.

You are special

First of all, let's get one thing straight, there is nobody on this planet who is exactly the same as you. There are many principles that apply to us all as members of the human race. For example, every person needs to move and fuel themselves to keep going – to what extent will vary for each individual. You are essentially the evolutionary dynamics that you have inherited from your parents and the genetically inherited strengths and weaknesses. The complex interaction of these factors ensures that each individual is born unique, although clearly similar to other people.

The concept of your body as a machine is the product of the thinking of philosophers such as Newton and Descartes and of the

Industrial Revolution, which envisioned a clockwork universe and man as a thinking machine. The way in which we fuel our machine, however, has deteriorated quite significantly. Current eating patterns are not making us any healthier.

Until a couple of hundred years ago, our ancestors had spent millions of years being hunter-gatherers and tens of thousands of years being peasant farmers, only to be propelled into the new towns and cities to fuel the need for labour during the Industrial Revolution. The diet the new industrial workers were fed consisted of fat, sugar and refined flour. A biscuit or a cake is a good example.

Flour was refined so that it would not go off, and cheap, energy-providing food was considered fuel in the same way that a car needs petrol. Not surprisingly, health declined. By about 1900, people had started to be smaller than in earlier generations. This led to the discovery of protein – the factor in food needed for growth. Sugar for energy, and protein for muscle. With this concept, the Western diet of high sugar, fat and protein was born.

Your body is an amazing machine, your heart beats, your blood goes around, your lungs breathe and your digestive system merrily gurgles away. Most of the time, especially when we are younger, we don't even need to think about all those bodily functions and we take them for granted. However, as we grow older, we become increasingly aware of how important it is to look after our bodies, especially as we are now living longer and physical preservation is a key consideration.

EXERCISE

Before delving into the subject of nutrition and diet, let's examine the concept of exercise. There really is no way around it: the lack of physical activity is probably the greatest reason why obesity figures are rising. However, there is no getting away from the fact that if you are overweight, you will feel tired, lethargic, suffer from digestive problems and have aching joints because your body has to take the strain of the extra load. A pill may take away the pain, but it does not get rid of the problem.

You need to increase your physical activity if you want to lose weight but exercise should not just be considered for weight loss alone – exercise is also good for your all-round health and well-being. As the biggest proportion of the population have non-physical jobs, it is easy to become disassociated from your body. Getting back in touch with it through exercise will increase your self-esteem and feelings of control, as well as your energy levels, metabolism and overall fitness. The chemicals and hormones that are released in the brain through exercise can help deal with stress and promote happiness.

I saw a strapline the other day that read: 'Energy – the more you give the more you get', which I think sums up exercise very well. People who exercise regularly are likely to live longer and enjoy a better quality of life. In fact, studies have shown that being physically unfit is just as dangerous as smoking in terms of lowering life expectancy.

How to get going

Sometimes the very mention of the word 'exercise' makes people want to reach for the chocolate. It can conjure up images of gyms, breathless running and crowded aerobics classes. And it puts many people off.

The good news is that you don't even have to go to a gym for hours and hours at a time. In reality, as little as half an hour of moderate

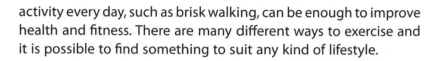

activity every day, such as brisk walking, can be enough to improve health and fitness. There are many different ways to exercise and it is possible to find something to suit any kind of lifestyle.

Be really honest with yourself now – at work do you walk up the stairs or take the lift? How many car journeys do you take door to door when really you could walk at least part of the way? Do you send an email when you could walk across the office to deliver the message in person? If you really sit and think about it, how active are you?

Here are a few suggestions on how to get more active.

- **Get a dog.** This is one of the best ways to get active. By taking it for a walk 3–4 times a day you will be really fit!

- **Volunteer.** Whether it's distributing food to the needy, helping elderly people, or participating in a fundraiser for a worthy cause in your community.

- **Rearrange your living room.** Move all your the furniture about and see how it looks. A new perspective can be energizing.

- **Go for a walk each morning and each evening.** Even if it's just for 20 minutes after work.

- **Take the stairs.** Climbing stairs is actually a great workout especially for your legs and bottom.

- **Give someone a massage.** This is one of the best ways to work with your hands.

- **Ride your bike to work.** If it's not too far away this is a great way to get some extra exercise.

- **Go swimming.** Swimming is one of the best ways to exercise and it is a great aerobic workout no matter what your physical shape.

- **Stretch each day.** Stretching helps to prevent muscle cramps and alleviates back pain as well as reducing stress.

Almost every function in our bodies depends partly on exercise for its optimum function: our digestion and elimination; our lungs and breathing; our heart and cardiovascular system; and, not least, our weight management.

Remember, too, that exercise is a positive investment for the future. While we worry about our pensions and make provision materially, it's worth considering whether we are going to be healthy and active enough in later life to enjoy our retirement. We are living longer these days – therefore our long-term health is of increasing concern.

Stay motivated: buy a pedometer

Recently I have discovered the wonders of a pedometer – a small device that you can clip on to your waistband to measure the number of steps you take each day. It is a great incentive and, by setting yourself a goal, you can measure and keep track of your objectives.

Wearing your pedometer to work will act as an additional incentive to keep you moving about. You can set yourself a specific number of steps that you would like to achieve at work. Encouraging your colleagues to wear one too will promote energy levels.

The pedometer makes expediency and functionality come together for a more accurate walking exercise.

It works through a sensor run by software attached to the apparatus. As you take a step forward and walk, the pedometer calculates your tread and every stride to provide you with a fairly accurate figure, regardless of a person's height. You can use whatever type of pedometer you like; there's one for every preference and lifestyle. If you are an office worker wanting to get out of the typical deskbound activity, you can walk around and perform some exercise without anyone noticing by means of purchasing a premium pedometer. For those who prefer aerobics and jogging, a pedometer that measures both jogging strides and aerobic moves is better.

Walking increases your heart-rate and ensures that your blood is being pumped around your body at a faster pace than when you are sitting still. The heart itself is a muscle and needs imposed exercise.

Government guidelines recommend that you should aim to walk 10,000 steps a day. It may sound a lot but 50 years ago this would have been the norm for every one of us. Today most overweight people are often walking less than 3000 steps per day and it is now estimated that we eat over twice as much as we did 50 years ago.

Walking is also the perfect antidote to depression and anxiety. It can aid the release of serotonin, a brain chemical that helps to rejuvenate your spirits. This is why so many people experience a natural high and lift in mood after exercising. It would be great if doctors could prescribe thirty minutes of brisk walking a day; this would be a very beneficial and positive self-medication.

Walking deserves special focus because it is often the easiest, most convenient and best exercise for many people.

You may not have an outrageously excessive diet; however, if you are not moving, you will put on weight. It's a very simple mathematical equation – calories in, versus calories out. You can try all the latest diet crazes in the world but, in the end, your success and failure will boil down to how you balance this simple equation.

NUTRITION

No matter who you are or where you live, the very fact that you are alive depends on you eating and keeping hydrated. Even the sight and smell of food can trigger the release of a pleasurable and rewarding chemical called dopamine in your brain.

However, while a delicious meal and a drink can be one of the most satisfying sensory experiences, it is also responsible for some of our greatest health problems.

You are essentially what you eat. Each human being is made up of roughly 63 per cent water, 22 per cent protein, 13 per cent fat and 2 per cent minerals and vitamins. Every single molecule comes from the food you eat and the water you drink. Eating the highest quality food in the right quantities helps you to achieve your highest potential for health, vitality and freedom from disease.

What is a well-balanced diet?

Nothing in Western society really teaches you to be healthy. Apart from any wisdom that your parents may impart, you may not really know how to be healthy. The media has embarked upon many well-intentioned health campaigns; but there are so many mixed messages – about what is good for you and what is not – that many people are left in a state of confusion about what constitutes a healthy, well-balanced diet.

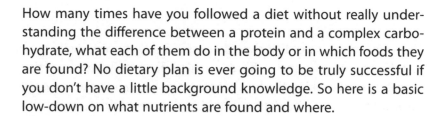

How many times have you followed a diet without really under-standing the difference between a protein and a complex carbo-hydrate, what each of them do in the body or in which foods they are found? No dietary plan is ever going to be truly successful if you don't have a little background knowledge. So here is a basic low-down on what nutrients are found and where.

Proteins

The word protein comes from the Greek word *protos* meaning 'first things'. Three quarters of all the solid matter in your body is protein, which forms the building blocks of our bodies. Without sufficient proteins, the body actually breaks down faster than it repairs itself.

Carbohydrates

There are two main types of carbohydrates: complex and simple. Basically, complex carbohydrates are those found in whole grains, and simple carbohydrates are those that have been processed and broken down.

Fats

The body needs a certain amount of fats for various vital functions. The brain and the nervous system are made up of around 60 per cent fats. All your hormones are created out of essential fats and the skin is lubricated and protected by them. Your skin is your largest bodily organ and is your first line of defence, so a lack of fats in your diet will actually show in dry scaly skin. Your skin is a great telltale sign of whether or not you are eating the right kind of fats.

Fibre

The ideal intake is not less than 35 grams a day. It is relatively easy to take in this amount of fibre – which absorbs water into the digestive tract making the food contents bulkier and easier to pass through the body – by eating whole grains, vegetables, fruit, nuts and seeds on a daily basis. Cereal fibre and linseed is especially good for avoiding constipation.

Vitamins

Although required in smaller amounts than fat, protein or carbohydrate, vitamins are extremely important to our diets. They stimulate enzymes which, in turn, make all the body processes happen. Vitamins are needed to balance hormones, produce energy, boost the immune system, make healthy skin and protect our arteries. They are also vital for our brain, nervous system and just about every body process.

Minerals

Like vitamins, minerals are essential. Calcium, magnesium and phosphorus help make up the bones and teeth. Nerve signals, which are vital for the brain and muscles, depend on calcium, magnesium, sodium and potassium. Other minerals include chromium for controlling blood sugar levels and selenium and zinc, which are essential for bodily repair and the immune system.

Water

Two-thirds of our bodies consist of water, which is therefore our most important nutrient. Water is the basis of all life and that includes your body. The muscles that move your body are 75 per cent water, the blood that transports nutrients is 82 per cent water, the lungs that provide your oxygen are 90 per cent water, and your brain – the control centre of your body – is 76 per cent water. Even your bones are 25 per cent water.

The body loses about 1.5 litres of water a day through the skin, lungs and via our kidneys through urine, ensuring that toxic substances are eliminated from the body. We also eliminate a third of a litre of water a day when glucose is burnt for energy. The ideal intake therefore is around 1.5 litres of water a day and more if you do more exercise. This is on top of water you may get through alkaline foods e.g. fruits and vegetables with high water content.

The biggest telltale sign of lack of hydration is low energy, headaches and irritability. Water can have a great effect on our energy at work and a suggestion is to keep a large bottle of water with you and try to set yourself a goal of drinking it all by the end of the day. Try it, it really does work wonders.

While we are surrounded with tempting media-hyped products packed full of sugar and other addictive flavourings, it is a challenge not to be tempted into overindulgence

There are certain foods and drinks that we would be best avoiding wherever possible.

Refined sugar

While cats like the taste of proteins, humans are principally attracted to the taste of carbohydrates – sweetness. The inherent attraction toward sweetness worked well for early man, because most things in nature that are sweet are not poisonous.

Unfortunately, however, we have learnt to extract the sweetness from nature and leave the goodness behind.

White sugar, for example, has 90 per cent of its vitamins and minerals removed. Without sufficient vitamins and minerals, our metabolism becomes inefficient contributing to poor health and weight management issues.

Sugary foods can also compromise your immune system. Research has shown that white blood cells are less efficient at fighting illness when exposed to refined sugar. A diet high in refined sugar will also raise your insulin levels quickly, which can lead to many other health problems. You will also lack energy as a result of these sugar spikes and the drop in blood sugar that follows.

Fruit contains a simpler and more natural sugar called fructose, which needs no digesting, but needs to be converted into glucose first. This slows down the metabolism, so you can balance your blood sugar levels more effectively. Keeping your blood sugar levels balanced is probably the most important factor in maintaining balanced even energy levels.

The average American consumes an astounding two to three pounds of sugar each week, which itself represents a huge increase over the last 20 years. Before 1900, the average consumption was only five pounds per person, per year.

In 2003, the United Nations and the World Health Organization released guidelines that sugar should account for no more than ten per cent of our daily calories. In a 2000-calorie-a-day diet, that's just 200 calories; or eight heaped teaspoons of table sugar at 25 calories each. A single can of fizzy drink is the equivalent of ten teaspoons, which would put you well over the recommended amount (and that is not to mention all the hidden refined sugars in processed food).

It's no secret that obesity and weight-related illnesses are on the rise in many countries and this is directly attributed to our diets and lifestyle. Our bodies simply aren't able to cope with such high sugar levels and this is why illnesses like diabetes and heart disease are at an all-time high. Cutting the excess sugar out of your diet is one of the best things you can do for your body.

Artificial sweeteners

When people decide to lose weight, one of the first changes many make to their diet is to add artificial sweeteners in place of sugar. We have been told by the government that artificial sweeteners are safe, but there are a great many indications – backed by current research – that suggest the contrary. Aspartame, for example, is made up of three components: 50 per cent is phenylalanine, 40 per cent is aspartic acid and 10 per cent is methanol or wood alcohol and was discovered as an ulcer drug, not a sweetener.

Alcohol

According to government guidelines, a healthy adult male can drink up to three units and a healthy adult female up to two units per day without harming their health. The latest suggestion is that would be well advised to have at least three or more alcohol-free days a week.

Caffeine

A day without a latte or a cup of tea or a caffeinated fizzy drink may seem unimaginable for some. However, caffeine is a drug, popularly consumed in coffee, tea, soft drinks and, in smaller doses, in chocolate. While we seem to have a love affair with these products, there's been quite a bit of confusion and even controversy surrounding caffeine lately. In moderation, caffeine is not too bad. However, many people become addicted to it (as it is a drug) and over- indulge – this is when it becomes harmful.

Understanding yourself and discovering what works best for you is the first step to better health and personal performance. There are, however, some key aspects of exercise and nutrition that are fundamental to all of us and this chapter is about helping you to raise awareness of the benefits of improving your health. Occasionally you may want to enjoy treats and give yourself permission to overindulge and be little bit lazy and that is perfectly acceptable . . . occasionally! It is important, however, that the underpinning framework for your life style is a well-balanced one. Successful lifestyle management is all about the healthy choices you make.

Fit for life: top tips

- ✓ Buy a pedometer and commit to doing 10,000 steps a day
- ✓ Make sure that you get out in the fresh air every day and walk
- ✓ Stand and stretch every 30 minutes – it is not good to sit for too long in one position
- ✓ Drink two litres of water a day (decaffeinated herbal teas count)
- ✓ Avoid drinking more than two cups of caffeinated coffee or three cups of caffeinated tea a day
- ✓ Have three alcohol-free days a week or more

✓ Avoid refined sugar and carbohydrates as much as possible
✓ Avoid artificial sweeteners and flavour enhancers
✓ Eat five portions of fresh fruit and vegetables a day
✓ Stick to approximately 2000 calories for a female and 2500 for a man –remember: calories in, versus calories out – so exercise more if you decide to overindulge in extra treats

If I'd known I was going to live so long, I'd have taken better care of myself.

Leon Eldred

4

DE-STRESS

Adopting the right attitude can convert a negative stress into a positive one

Hans Selye

One day a young woman called Penny accompanied her husband Lawrence to the doctor's office because he had been suffering with headaches and lack of sleep. He seemed especially irritable and generally out of sorts. After Lawrence had completed his check-up, the doctor called Penny into his office alone.

He told her: 'Your husband is suffering from high levels of stress. If you don't do the following, he will surely need to be hospitalized.'

'What can I do to help him?' asked Penny.

The doctor continued, 'To help reduce his stress each morning you must get up before him and fix him a healthy breakfast. Be pleasant at all times. Prepare him a nutritious packed lunch. When he comes home from work greet him with a happy smile, do not burden him with chores. Do not discuss your problems with him, as it will only make his stress worse. There must be absolutely no nagging. You must also give him any amount of affection he requires, whenever he demands it. If you can do this for the next ten months to a year, I think it will help to reduce his stress levels and he could well regain his health completely.'

On the way home, Lawrence who was very concerned asked Penny, 'What did the doctor say to you?'

To which Penny responded, 'He said it looks like you are going to be hospitalized.'

****

Stress most certainly seems to be the modern-day dilemma. Pretty much every organization I work with – in whichever country – experiences high levels of stress-related illness amongst their staff. According to the American Psychological Association (APA), one-third of Americans are living with extreme stress and nearly half of

Americans believe that their stress levels have increased over the past five years.

I think it would be fair to say that a little bit of pressure can be constructive, it can even galvanize you and help you to perform better at something. However, too much pressure or prolonged pressure can lead to stress, which is unhealthy for the mind and body. Everyone reacts differently to stress, and some people may have a higher threshold than others. Too much stress can often lead to physical, mental and emotional problems.

Anxiety and depression are the most common mental health issues and the majority of cases are caused by stress. Research by mental health charities also suggests that a quarter of the population will have a mental health problem at some point in their lives.

WHAT IS STRESS?

Stress is your body's way of responding to any kind of demand or pressure. It can be caused by both positive and negative experiences. When faced with a situation that makes you stressed, your body releases chemicals, including cortisol, adrenaline and noradrenaline.

These chemicals give people more energy and strength, which can be a good thing if their stress is caused by physical danger. This, however, can also be a bad thing if their stress is in response to something emotional and there is no outlet for this extra energy and strength.

Many different things can cause stress. Identifying what may be causing them is the first step in learning how to cope. Some of the most common sources of stress are listed below.

Survival stress

You may have heard the phrase 'fight or flight'; this is a common response to danger in all people and animals. When you are afraid that someone or something may be trying to hurt you, your body naturally responds with a burst of energy so that you will be better able to survive the dangerous situation (fight) or escape it altogether (flight).

Internal stress

Have you ever worried about things that have happened that you can do nothing about and that you have absolutely no control over? We all do, I am sure, from time to time. This is internal stress and it is one of the most important kinds of stress to understand and manage. Internal stress is when people make themselves stressed and anxious.

Stress releases certain chemicals into your system that can be highly addictive and some people become 'stress junkies' by getting off on a chemical high. They may even look for stressful situations and feel stressed about things that aren't stressful. This, for some people, is like coffee – a stimulant that acts as false energy and motivation.

Environmental stress

This is a response to things around you that cause stress, such as noise, crowding and pressure from work or family. Identifying these environmental stresses and learning to avoid them or deal with them will help lower your stress level. Certainly some people are more sensitive to this than others and find it more difficult to filter out environmental distractions.

Workplace stress

This kind of stress builds up over a long time and can take its toll on your body. It can be caused by working too much or too hard and not getting your work–home balance into a healthy perspective. Not knowing how to manage your time well, or how to take time out for rest and relaxation can also be a cause. It can be one of the hardest kinds of stress to avoid because many people perceive it as out of their control.

Stress can affect both your body and your mind. People under large amounts of stress can become tired, sick, and unable to concentrate or think clearly. Sometimes, stress can even trigger severe depression and mental breakdowns.

In our fast-paced society, the term stress-related burnout seems almost to go with the territory. It certainly appears to be an ever-present reality. Technology can have a big influence here. Mobile phones – and a whole host of other progressive technologies – are useful in some ways and a curse in others. People find it harder these days to switch off.

Clearly, the rising figures of stress-related illness are very concerning for many organizations, who keep the interest and well-being of their people at the heart of their business. Many employers attempt to provide a stress-free work environment and identify where it is becoming a problem for staff, and have strategies in place to deal with it. Some, unfortunately, have not recognized the importance of doing this.

Stress in the workplace reduces productivity, increases management pressures and makes people ill in many ways. It also creates a serious risk of litigation for all employers and organizations, carrying significant liabilities for damages, bad publicity and loss of reputation. What is more, dealing with stress-related claims consumes vast amounts of management time. Clearly, then, there are strong economic and financial reasons for organizations to manage and reduce stress at work, aside from the obvious humanitarian and ethical considerations.

SYMPTOMS AND CAUSES

Many factors can trigger stress and some of the symptoms include headaches, lack of concentration, muscle tension, body overheating, shivering, rashes, depression, upset stomach, cramps, irritability, constant mind chatter, mood swings, emotional outburst and various other things.

If you have been experiencing some of these symptoms for a long period of time you are at risk of developing high blood pressure which can lead to heart attacks and stroke.

Experiencing even one or two of these symptoms can make you feel frustrated or anxious, and this can be a vicious circle. For example, you want to avoid stress but symptoms such as frequent crying or mind chatter can make you feel annoyed with yourself and even more stressed.

I did some research a few years ago around stress in the workplace and one of my key findings in terms of what stresses people at work was 'other people'. It's interesting how other people can make us feel stressed, either because we catch their 'stress germs' or, perhaps, they become the audience that we create in our minds, which sits in judgement upon our every action. Very often we will have a perception of what we believe people expect from us and, in some cases, we put ourselves under unnecessary pressure trying to meet an expectation that was never there in the first place.

There is a danger that we can put self-imposed pressures upon ourselves because we are so concerned about what people think of us. This is where self-esteem is so important and, hopefully, the advice in Chapters One and Two will have been useful in helping you to develop your self-confidence.

Here are a few suggestions for things that you can do to cope with stress.

1 Mind chatter

One of the best ways to tackle stress is to address your mind chatter. When the subconscious mind is told something by the conscious mind it doesn't distinguish between what is real and what is artificial. It will believe whatever you tell it. Therefore, if you tell yourself that you are stressed, then you will be. The danger is sometimes stress can become a habit and you may attach a way of thinking to a certain set of circumstances. For example, if you were stressed in a certain situation in the past, then you might talk yourself into believing that you will be again; so then it becomes a self-fulfilling prophecy.

I have certainly worked in environments where stress is almost fashionable, where people are rushing around like headless chickens, telling everyone how stressed they are rather than getting on with the things that are stressing them out. I also think that some people 'big up' their stress levels to demonstrate how busy they are.

That kind of culture tends to breed an epidemic of stress, because everyone else then thinks that they should be stressed too. Actually working smarter, not harder, is by far the best way to prevent stress – and also to listen to yourself and recognize the difference.

It is very easy to blame anything and everything around you for the stress you are feeling. In fact, stress has become such a convenient scapegoat that it can easily prevent you from taking responsibility for seeking a different approach to your work that could create a more successful work ethos. Whenever you feel stress, challenge the way that you go about things.

2 Worry less

Worry comes from the Anglo Saxon word 'wyrgan' which means to strangle and choke until there is no life left. The danger with worrying is that it is a bit like a rocking chair. It gives you something to do, but it rarely gets you anywhere. The danger, too, is that as you worry you end up creating stressful outcomes in your mind, which just feeds and perpetuates your negative thoughts.

3 Embrace change

One of the things that can really stress people out is change. We tend to be creatures of habit and we like things to remain the same, because change requires some initial effort and flexibility. However, in an ever-evolving world change is inevitable, and keeping an open and positive mind – whilst focusing on the positive benefits that those changes can bring – can only help us to seek out opportunities and personal growth. I will cover more about embracing change in the next chapter.

4 Be more assertive

Assertiveness is a great communication skill to develop, especially when we simply do not have enough time on our hands and we have to say no to a request. Also, if you are a passive or aggressive communicator, poor communication skills can add to your stress levels.

One of the issues that we have sometimes, especially when we want to be perceived as positive and hardworking, is to say no when we have too much on our plates. However, we have to be realistic for our own sanity. It may be that you are able to do part of something but not all of it. So, before you jump in with a definite yes or no, assess the situation and negotiate a positive win–win outcome for all concerned.

5 Manage anger

The term 'anger management' is widely used now, and celebrities with volatile temperaments regular make the news. It is clearly something that affects people in the workplace, especially when it manifests itself through stress. However, anger management is simply one aspect of handling pressure, since anger in the workplace is just one of many symptoms of stress.

Anger is often stress in denial and, as such, is best approached via one-to-one counselling. Training courses can usefully convey anger-management and stress-reduction theory and ideas, but one-to-one counselling is necessary to turn theory into practice. Management of anger (and any other difficult emotional behaviour for that matter) and the stress that causes it, can only be improved if a person wants to change by acceptance, cognizance and commitment. Awareness is the first requirement.

Establishing commitment to change – and identifying the causes – is sufficient for many people to make adjustments and improve. The will to change, combined with awareness of causes, then leads to a solution.

6 Develop healthier eating habits

As we have covered in the previous chapter it is very important to eat a healthy, balanced diet – especially when you are stressed – because food and drink can have a big impact on the way that you feel and act. Some people find that stress causes them to snack on sugary, unhealthy foods such as crisps and biscuits. This gives your body a sugar rush followed by a sharp drop in sugar and energy levels. This can make you feel tired or irritable, as well as making it harder for you to concentrate.

Eating at regular times and not skipping meals can make a big difference. This allows your body to release a steady stream of energy throughout the day, which will help improve your concentration and mood.

It's widely accepted that nutritional deficiency impairs the health of the body, and it's unrealistic not to expect the brain to be affected as well by poor diet. If the brain is affected, so are our thoughts, feelings and behaviour.

A proper, balanced diet is clearly essential, both to avoid direct physical stress causes via brain and nervous system, and to reduce stress susceptibility as a result of poor health and condition. Processed foods are not as good for you as fresh natural foods. Look at all the chemicals listed on the packaging to see what you are putting into your body.

The rule is simple and inescapable: eat and drink healthily, avoid excessive intake of toxins, and this will reduce stress and stress susceptibility. If you are suffering from stress and not obeying this simple rule, you will continue to be stressed and, moreover, you will maintain a higher susceptibility to stress.

Irrespective of your tastes, it's easy these days to have a balanced healthy diet if you want to – the challenge isn't in knowing what's good and bad, it's simply a matter of commitment and personal resolve. You have one body for the whole of your life – look after it.

Avoid caffeine

Caffeine can exacerbate or even cause stress, anxiety, depression and insomnia because it interferes with a tranquilizing neurotransmitter chemical in the brain called adenosine. This is the chemical which turns down our anxiety levels – it's our body's version of a tranquilizer. Caffeine docks into a receptor for adenosine, and regular use of caffeine is enough to produce anxiety and depression in susceptible individuals.

Research has indicated that caffeine increases the secretion of stress hormones like adrenaline. So, if you are already secreting higher stress hormones, caffeine will boost them further and exacerbate stress/anxiety or depression. By cutting your caffeine intake you will lower your stress hormone levels and reduce stress, anxiety and depression.

Reduce alcohol

Now you may see a glass of wine at the end of a hard day as a great stress reliever. However, think again. Alcohol, when consumed in large amounts, stimulates the hypothalamus, adrenal and pituitary glands. One result of this is an increased level of both cortisol and adrenaline within the body. Both play a significant role in reinforcing the symptoms of stress.

7 Exercise more

The benefits of exercise are numerous, as I hope I have already expressed in the previous chapter. Not only does it release a chemical called serotonin, which makes you feel happier and less stressed, it also improves circulation and prevents conditions such as stroke and heart attack. Exercise also allows you to take out your frustration and anger in a constructive way through a very positive channel.

In particular, fast walking has been found to be very beneficial for relieving stress, as well as being an effective method of weight control.

8 Sleep well

It is common for your sleep patterns to be disturbed when you are feeling stressed. If you are worried about something, it can often be on your mind even when you try to forget about it. This may cause sleepless nights or bad dreams. You may find it difficult getting to sleep or you may wake up a few times during the night. Feeling under pressure can also make you tired and groggy the next day, which can make you feel even more stressed. In fact, sleep deprivation is itself a cause of stress. Here are a few tips to help you sleep better.

- **Go to bed and get up at about the same time every day, even on the weekends.** Sticking to a schedule helps reinforce

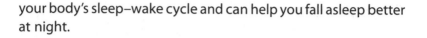

your body's sleep–wake cycle and can help you fall asleep better at night.

● **Avoid eating or drinking large amounts before bedtime.** Eat a light dinner about two hours before sleeping.

● **Exercise regularly.** Regular physical activity, especially aerobic exercise, can help you fall asleep faster and make your sleep more restful. Don't exercise within three hours of your bedtime, however. Exercising right before bed may make getting to sleep more difficult.

● **Make your bedroom cool, dark, quiet and comfortable.** Create a room that's ideal for sleeping. Adjust the lighting, temperature, humidity and noise level to your preferences. Use blackout curtains, eye covers, earplugs, extra blankets, a fan, a humidifier or other devices to create an environment that suits your needs.

● **Choose a comfortable mattress and pillow.** Features of a good bed are subjective and differ for each person. But make sure you have a bed that's comfortable. If you share your bed, make sure there's enough room for two. Children and pets are often disruptive, so you may need to set limits on how often they sleep in bed with you.

● **Start a relaxing bedtime routine.** Do the same things each night to tell your body it's time to wind down. This may include taking a warm bath or shower, reading a book, or listening to soothing music. Relaxing activities done with lowered lights can help ease the transition between wakefulness and sleepiness.

● **Use sleeping pills only as a last resort.** Check with your doctor before taking any sleep medications.

9 Laugh more

Humour is one of the greatest and quickest devices for reducing stress. It works because laughter produces helpful chemicals in the brain. Humour also gets your brain thinking and working in a different way – it distracts you from having a stressed mindset. Distraction is a simple effective de-stressor – it takes your thoughts away from the stress, and thereby diffuses the stressful feelings.

Therefore, most people will feel quite different and notice a change in mindset after laughing and being distracted by something humorous. Here are a few tips to help you laugh more:

- **Laugh at yourself.** When you think about laughter and how you can bring more of it into your life, remember to spend some time laughing at yourself. We all do silly things or embarrassing things and one of the best ways to turn a negative into a positive is to laugh about it.

- **Watch a funny TV show.** This is one of the easiest ways to cultivate a funny environment. There are a lot of great TV shows and films filled with comedic relief.

- **Go to a comedy club.** Even better than watching funny people on TV is actually going to a comedy show. Have you ever been to one? If not, I'd highly recommend it. Comedians are so clever, and just by being in that kind of environment is good.

- **Help people to laugh at themselves.** Sometimes other people forget to laugh at themselves. Some people forget that you can choose to laugh, even when you feel like crying. You can help people out by helping them realize that it's sometimes better to see the funny side of life.

● **Find the funny side.** Sometimes when we are faced with very serious situations, it can be very hard to see the good in them, let alone the funny side. If you have the will you can always find the humorous silver lining in every situation.

10 Have a good cry!

I call this the detoxification of the soul. When you are feeling really tense or stressed, a good cry can work wonders. This is often easier for women than men. Not much is known about the physiology of crying and tears, although many find that crying – weeping proper tears – has a powerful, helpful effect on stress levels. Whatever the science behind crying, a good bout of sobbing and weeping does seem to release tension for many people.

It is a shame that attitudes towards crying and tears prevent many people from crying, and it's a sad reflection on our unforgiving society that some people who might benefit from a good cry feel that they shouldn't do it ever – even in complete privacy. Unfortunately, most of us – especially boys – are told as children that crying is bad or shameful or childish, which is utter nonsense in my opinion.

Shedding a few tears can be a very good thing now and then, and if you've yet to discover its benefits then give it a try and see how it makes you feel. You might be surprised.

11 Breathe deeply

If you feel yourself getting stressed, try to halt those feelings in their tracks by relaxing your muscles and taking deep breaths. Start by inhaling for three seconds, then exhale for a little longer.

This will help to remove the older oxygen from your lungs and replace it with fresh oxygen that will improve your circulation and alertness. Continue these deep breathing exercises until you feel calmer and ready to continue what you were doing. It might be better to do something else rather than continue with the stressful task.

12 Take time to relax

When you are stressed, your muscles often tense, which can cause muscular aches to develop later on. When you feel yourself getting stressed, shrug your shoulders a few times and shake out your arms and legs. This will help to loosen your muscles. During the course of a day, stressful events as well as poor postures will tighten many of the 60,000 muscles in your body. Tensed muscles often remain tightened and do not automatically relax. Tensed muscles trigger irritability, which tenses more muscles in a vicious cycle. You can learn exercises, which can help. A relaxed body reduces the prospect of anger, or despair, and will reduce the symptoms of stress. Some people find that it helps them to relax if they imagine a peaceful place, such as a desert island or a tranquil lake. Imagine yourself being there and the scenery around you. Diverting your mind to a calming environment will help to distract you from the stress, and relax your body.

Whatever you decide to do, it is really important to give yourself time to switch off and chill out to avoid burn out. You need to make sure that you do not drive yourself too hard. Stress can take its toll on the body and the mind and have far-reaching consequences. When you feel yourself getting stressed, it is far better to down tools and focus on what you are going to do to alleviate the symptoms. Exploring what works best for you will enable you to avoid getting upset or ill and will help you to feel more in control.

De-stress: top tips

✓ Listen to your internal chatter and avoid self-imposed stress
✓ Be positive about change and seek out the benefits
✓ Be more assertive in the way that you communicate and deal with things
✓ Manage you time more effectively and manage your personal efficiency
✓ Learn how to manage your emotions and try see the light-hearted side
✓ Eat a health balanced diet and avoid too much caffeine and alcohol
✓ Get out in the fresh air, go for a walk and get some exercise
✓ Make sure that you get good quality sleep 6–8 hours every night
✓ Take deep breaths and focus on controlling your breathing
✓ Explore relaxation techniques and take time out every day just for you

Take rest; a field that has rested gives a bountiful crop.

Ovid

5

MANAGING CHANGE

*It is not the strongest of the species that survives,
or the most intelligent, but rather the one most
adaptable to change*

Charles Darwin

One day, a man called Nicholas found a small butterfly cocoon. He decided to keep it so that he could watch the metamorphosis of the butterfly, as he had never seen this event before. Nicholas put the cocoon carefully on his desk and the next day a small opening appeared. For several hours, he sat and watched the butterfly as it struggled to force its body through the little hole. Then it seemed to stop making any progress. It appeared to be stuck.

Nicholas decided to help the butterfly and, with a pair of scissors, he cut open the cocoon. The butterfly then emerged easily. Something was strange, however.

He looked closer and noticed that the butterfly had a swollen body and shrivelled wings. Nicholas watched the butterfly, expecting it to take on its correct proportions.

Nothing happened and the butterfly stayed the same. Sadly it was never able to fly.

In his kindness and haste Nicholas did not realize that the butterfly's struggle to get through the small opening of the cocoon is nature's way of forcing fluid from the body of the butterfly into its wings so that it would be ready for flight.

Like the sapling which grows strong from being buffeted by the wind, in life we all need to struggle sometimes to make us stronger.

****

The change process can sometimes be a struggle, but our ability to be strong and manage change positively and confidently is becoming an increasingly important life skill. Change can bring about all sorts of reactions in people. Some positively embrace

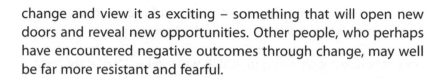

change and view it as exciting – something that will open new doors and reveal new opportunities. Other people, who perhaps have encountered negative outcomes through change, may well be far more resistant and fearful.

When dealing with change it is so important not to allow negative baggage from the past to cloud our perspective. An acknowledgement of what we may have to let go of is important. However, a focus on all the things we will gain is by far the best approach. An acceptance, too, that we will experience a range of emotions through the process is sensible. One inevitable fact of life is that things do change; so learning to go with the flow, and riding the crest of the wave, will be make the journey far more enjoyable, interesting and positive.

CHANGE AND MODERN LIVING

Life in the twenty tens has seemingly propelled us into a rapidly evolving world, where the escalating pace of change is greater today than at any other time in our recorded history. Every aspect of our lives is changing, including the way that we work, the way that we communicate, the way that we shop and eat and, for the majority, the entire way that we live our day to day lives

In contrast to the past, it is frequently the norm to change not only our jobs, but our entire careers, several times. People now think nothing of relocating, not only within their own country but also internationally. And it is increasingly common for people to be married more than once and to have more than one family. It's as if we are trying to fit several lifetimes into one.

Never before have so many of us needed to deal with so many life-changing decisions, in so many different areas, on such a consistent and accelerating basis. So, one of the great challenges of our times is the ability to cope with change.

Let's face it, the only thing of which we can be absolutely certain is that there will be continuing change in all of our lives. At times, the changes may only be minor while, at other times, they will be major, but all of us will experience some degree of change. It is inevitable. You cannot stop it! You cannot even slow it down or delay it. What you can do however, with a little knowledge, skill and effort, is to learn how to manage it.

Change is, in fact, a vital criterion for any form of evolution or growth, whether as individuals or as an entire community, society, country or world. Without change there can be no movement or growth, either personal or global.

Just as nature is in an ongoing cycle of change, so we, as part of nature, are constantly changing. Continuing change is not only a certainty of life but also necessary for our own growth, evolution and general well-being.

CHANGE AND GRIEF

It is important to understand the relationship between change and grief. No matter how positive change experience or outcome may be, it still means loss. When something changes, you lose the old way of being or the old set of circumstances, and a certain amount of grief is inevitable.

Many years ago, people with terminal illnesses were an embarrassment for doctors. Someone who could not be cured was evidence of the doctors' fallibility and, as a result, the doctors regularly shunned the dying with the excuse that there was nothing more that could be done.

Elizabeth Kübler-Ross was a psychiatrist in Switzerland who challenged this unkindness, and spent a lot of time with dying people – both comforting and studying them. She wrote a book, called *On Death and Dying*, which included a cycle of emotional states that is often referred to as the 'grief cycle'.

Her observation was that this emotional cycle was not exclusive to the terminally ill, but also other people who were affected by a change that was perceived to be negative.

The basic grief cycle model has been developed by many organizations to help examine the emotional rollercoaster that people experience when they face change. Some general key stages include:

- **Shock** – which can be the initial paralysis at hearing the bad news

- **Denial** – which is very common when people are trying to avoid the inevitable

- **Anger** – which can be caused by frustration and an outpouring of bottled-up emotion

- **Bargaining** – which is about looking for a way out, or an alternative

- **Depression** – when the reality is perceived as a negative one

- **Acceptance** – when people are ready to move forward

A common problem with the cycle is that people get stuck in one phase. They may get stuck in denial, never moving on from the position of non-acceptance. This might occur when a person loses their job, but they make the journey to work anyway, only to sit on a park bench all day.

Getting stuck in denial is common in 'cool' cultures where expressing anger is not acceptable. The person may feel the anger, but they repress and bottle it up, which is not healthy.

Understanding the grief cycle can help us to map out where we are when we experience change, and why we are feeling the emotion. It can also help us to be more empathetic with others when they react in a certain way. The key is to be aware of it. However, like any negative or damaging emotion, we need to move through it as positively and quickly as we can. We cannot change anything until we accept it.

Condemnation does not liberate, it oppresses.

Carl Jung

Focusing on the rewards that change can bring will be very helpful.

THE BENEFITS OF CHANGE

People in every age have learned how to benefit from the winds of change – great leaders, inventors, pioneers, innovators and builders. In fact, every great success, in any area of life, will have been achieved in some way through learning to adapt successfully to change and embracing the potential it can bring.

The paradox sometimes is that though we want something to get better, we are not prepared to come out of our comfort zone and make the necessary changes to achieve it. Sometimes we need to grasp the nettle and go for it. There is a great quote by Henry Ford who said: 'If you always do what you've always done, you'll always get what you've always got'. I mean, let's face it, if life always stayed the same and nothing ever changed wouldn't it get a bit boring?

There are so many benefits to change, and it is important to focus on these when things feel a bit daunting. So, here are a few examples of the benefits of change.

● Change can help you to be more versatile and learn to go with the flow, which is sometimes a positive thing to do.

● Change can help you to learn to be more flexible – and blessed are the flexible, for they shall not be bent out of shape! Change can make you a lot smarter. If things never changed, you would never learn anything new. Every time you learn a new skill, even if it is just how to be better at adapting, you are that much smarter than you were yesterday. Change reminds us that anything is possible. It is so easy to get stuck sometimes, perhaps in a job you don't like, a home you feel uncomfortable in, or maybe in a relationship you are not happy in. When you see things change, whether It is in your life or someone else's, it's encouraging to know that nothing stays the same forever. Change brings about growth and the opportunity to create new approaches to problem solving and solution finding, which is very useful with some of the challenges we face today.

● Change challenges and reduces the status-quo mentality, and can facilitate growth in a positive way.

● Change can help us to respond better to negative internal and external driving forces.

Most of all, change provides us with new opportunities and paves the way for greater things. The more open minded we are, the more we can embrace the benefits.

MANAGING CHANGE

Managing personal change starts with a clear understanding of what our unconscious or hidden commitments and values really are. This will be the biggest stumbling block to being open and receptive to change. From early childhood onwards, we all develop our own inner map of reality and we understand, interpret and relate to the world 'out there' through this inner map.

Our capacity to be conscious or aware of our own inner map, and especially how we create our experience of life through it, is determined by our level of self-awareness. Raising our levels of self-awareness (as we looked at in Chapter Two) is a very useful thing to work on.

However, for most of us, most of the time, the way we perceive our world is an unconscious process and, in accordance with this inner map, we have our own inner commitments to our own personal priorities. These will have been built up over the years and the negative and positive experiences that we have.

Our hidden, inner commitments have a high priority and will override any counter intentions that conflict with them. We assign this a high priority because the hidden commitment is inextricably linked to an inner hidden perception that we have of our own physical, psychological, social or emotional safety and requirements. This hidden commitment is nearly always outside of our conscious awareness.

The quickest and easiest way to identify our inner resistance is to observe our reactions and our behaviour in our attempts to change. Making notes of how you react in certain situations will help you to be able to process the information so that you can understand yourself better. Personal intelligence is the most valuable form of intelligence and will provide you with the information you need to decide what you want to change.

Every change, big or small, has some impact. Sometimes the issue with change is that it has a cluster effect. One change often seems to be followed by several more, and it can feel as though your whole world is changing.

Learning how to manage change more effectively will help you to be better equipped and more positive when it happens to you. So here are a few things to consider.

1 Embrace change

This quote by Leo Tolstoy is something to reflect upon: 'It seldom happens that a man changes his life through his habitual reasoning. No matter how fully he may sense the new plans and aims revealed to him by reason, he continues to plod along in old paths until his life becomes frustrating and unbearable — he finally makes the change only when his usual life can no longer be tolerated.' Sadly, I think this is frequently true – we procrastinate in order to put off the inevitable. The danger is that we are wasting precious time in our lives being unhappy when we could turn it all around by embracing change.

2 Be open minded

Your mind is like a parachute: it works best when it is open. Sometimes we can drag the baggage of the past and superimpose it onto situations without being open minded and taking a fresh perspective. One thing that I hear a great deal from people who resist change is 'Well we tried that before and it didn't work'. Every situation is different and just because something didn't work last time it doesn't mean it won't work this time.

3 Prepare your emotions

Accept the fact that you may be emotional during the change process. In the face of change you may feel unhappy, fearful, inse-cure, unsettled, frustrated. On the other side of the table, however, you may feel enthusiastic, elated, delighted and excited. Any of those emotions will have an impact on your energy levels so it is really important to prepare yourself.

4 Relax and go with the flow

Sometimes change happens and we have absolutely no control over it whatsoever. When this occurs, you have to choose how you are going to respond. If you resist change and remain rigid and inflexible it will be a lot more difficult and even painful. Going with the flow sometimes is the best approach. It may help to think of yourself as a boat in a storm. If you turn against the waves they will crush you, if you go with them they will carry you home.

5 Be positive

Having a positive attitude to change is the right mindset to culti-vate. If we go into a change situation believing that it is negative then we are more likely to experience negative outcomes. Whilst it is important to understand some of the risks and pitfalls involved, it is also important to focus on positive outcomes.

6 Keep calm and carry on

This old war expression is very apt. Some people literally panic when change happens because it totally destabilizes their world. If change is happening to you and it's quite big then keep up as many familiar things as you can as a reminder of how much there is in your life that isn't changing. Stick to your usual routines, see people you normally see, and reassure yourself that not every-thing has to change just because some things have.

7 Get support

You don't need to try to cope alone or keep your feelings to your-self. This can actually be very unhelpful, repressing emotion can cause stress. Talk about it, have a hug, try to see the light-hearted side of the situation and get a bit of reassurance. 'Being brave' doesn't really win you any awards these days and will always mean managing your issues alone. It may mean finding the courage to ask for help. However, a supportive friend can be the very best tonic and help you to get another perspective.

8 Challenge your perspective

Sometimes the way we view a situation can be very narrow because we are perceiving it through our own set of filters and will, perhaps, benchmark it against our previous experiences. It is important to really examine the situation from all angles. Be careful not to get yourself stuck up a one-way street with your thinking. There is always another angle and another perspective.

9 Chunk up change

If you are dealing with a big change, try to divide the larger pieces into smaller steps where possible. For instance, a house move, a wedding or a divorce involves several stages. When you feel overwhelmed by the enormity of the change, concentrate on the step you've reached, rather than the bigger picture.

10 Make a plan

Change can overwhelm us, especially when our minds race and we start to imagine all of the things that could happen. We begin to catastrophize and, before we know it, we are feeling completely out of control. A good way to regain control and settle our minds is to make a plan of what we are going to do. Prepare a contingency. Write it all down so that you can actually see it. Very often it's what we don't know and we can't see that scares us the most, especially those of us with wild and vivid imaginations.

11 Keep the end in mind

Change, as the butterfly experiences, can be painful. You may have heard the expression 'What doesn't kill you makes you stronger' and sometimes we need to experience some pain in order to really relish and appreciate the reward. As change occurs and we experience discomfort it is also important to remind ourselves that this time will pass. All change comes to an end when the new circumstances are in place and become familiar to you. Every change, no matter how big, will end and you'll return to a feeling of normality.

CHANGE AND OTHERS

One thing that it is important to understand is that trying to change others can be an invidious task. Sometimes we can get frustrated with people, whether it's family, relationships, or people we work with. However, if we expend too much energy creating an expectation of how we want someone to be, and then to try and go about changing them, we will set ourselves up for a great deal of disappointment. Focusing on others' strengths, and constructively feeding back information that may help them, may be beneficial. Be careful, however, that you are not expending too much energy on other people when you could be improving and changing yourself. Best to be the change you want, and encourage others through action and example.

There will be occasions in your life where you are the catalyst for change, and it may be that you need to direct and support others, and this can be quite challenging, especially when you experience resistance. Having a clear understanding about how change feels will give you immediate empathy so that is a good starting point.

The toughest challenge for change agents can be managing expectations. The secret can be found in constant communication. There will be times that you will have to give direction more than once and more than one way. Being aware that some people will be experiencing the fear factor will help you to put your message across in a way that will diffuse anxiety.

Highlighting the benefits is a good way of helping people to see the possibilities that lie ahead, and to encourage people to get on board. However, it is also important to satisfy the realists and people with a more pessimistic approach, otherwise they may feel railroaded and uncomfortable. An examination and acknowledgement of the risk aspects needs to be addressed.

So, one thing that is inevitable is that every one of us will experience change. For some it will be easier than for others and we will all deal with it in different ways. Resisting change that we have no control over can potentially be harmful, so learning how to navigate our way through stormy waters is very useful. We also need to take responsibility for how we respond and how this can affect others. If we demonstrate the courage to embrace change we will be giving those who may struggle the strength and support they may need.

It is also very useful to remember this: if you don't like something, change it; if you can't change it, change the way you think about it. You are far more in control than you may think.

Manage change: top tips

✓ Embrace change to get the best and most out of life
✓ Be open-minded to all the opportunities that change can bring
✓ Understand the emotions that change can evoke and mentally prepare yourself
✓ Understand the key stages of the grieving process that may affect you
✓ Relax and go with the flow when you cannot control a situation
✓ Be positive and seek out and focus on the benefits of change

✓ Keep calm and carry on and manage change more practically
✓ Read up and get inspired by success stories of people who experienced change
✓ Chunk up change to make it easier and plan a contingency
✓ Get support from others and talk about how you feel to get another perspective

Be the change you want the world to be

Mahatma Gandhi

6

BOUNCE ABILITY

*It's not how far you fall, it's how high you bounce
when you reach the bottom.*

Author Unknown

A young woman called Sara went to visit her mother Elizabeth one day because she was feeling fed up and miserable. Sara had recently been told that her job was going to be made redundant, money was tight and she had just split up with her boyfriend. Sara told her mother that she was tired of fighting and struggling and felt like just giving up.

Her mother listened patiently, and then told her daughter Sara that she wanted to show her something, and took her into the kitchen. She proceeded to fill three saucepans with water and placed them on the hob to boil.

In the first saucepan, she placed carrots, in the second she placed eggs, and in the last she placed ground coffee beans.

They both stayed in contemplative silence and watched them boil away. About fifteen minutes later Elizabeth turned off the burners. She fished the carrots out and placed them in a bowl. She pulled the eggs out and placed them in a bowl. Then she ladled the coffee out and placed it in a bowl.

Turning to her daughter, Elizabeth asked, 'Tell me, what do you see?'

'Carrots, eggs, and coffee', Elizabeth replied.

Elizabeth brought her closer and asked her to feel the carrots. Sara did so and noted that they were soft. Elizabeth then asked her daughter to take an egg and break it. After pulling off the shell, she observed the hard-boiled egg. Finally, Elizabeth asked her to sip the coffee. Sara smiled as she tasted its rich aroma.

Sara then asked her mother 'What are you trying to show me?'

Elizabeth explained that although each of these objects had faced the same adversity by being submerged in boiling water, each one had reacted differently.

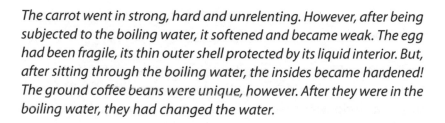

The carrot went in strong, hard and unrelenting. However, after being subjected to the boiling water, it softened and became weak. The egg had been fragile, its thin outer shell protected by its liquid interior. But, after sitting through the boiling water, the insides became hardened! The ground coffee beans were unique, however. After they were in the boiling water, they had changed the water.

'Which are you?' Elizabeth asked her daughter. 'When adversity knocks on your door, how do you respond? Are you a carrot, an egg, or a coffee bean?'

Sara looked puzzled, so Elizabeth suggested that she asked herself the following questions:

- *Am I the carrot that seems strong but, with pain and adversity, do I wilt and become soft and lose my strength?*

- *Am I the egg that starts with a malleable heart, but changes with the heat? Did I have a fluid spirit but, after a loss, a breakup, or a financial hardship, does my shell look the same, but on the inside am I bitter and tough with a stiff spirit and a hardened heart?*

- *Or am I like the coffee bean? The bean actually changes the hot water, the very circumstance that brings the pain. When the water gets hot, it releases the fragrance and flavour. If you are like the bean, when things are at their worst, you get better and change the situation around you.*

When the hours are the darkest and trials are their greatest, do you elevate to another level?

****

So, how do you handle adversity? Are you a carrot, an egg, or a coffee bean?

Having the ability to bounce back from some of the challenges that we face is not only useful it is becoming increasingly necessary in a world where we are faced with so many challenges. Personal resilience seems to be high up on the agenda when it comes to coping with modern living.

I can most certainly vouch for the benefits of developing 'bounce ability'. Being able to pick yourself up and dust yourself off and carry on is an essential skill for a happy life. It is key to survival. You may have heard the expression 'survival of the fittest'; I would be more inclined to say 'survival of the most bouncy'. The quicker that you can recover from life's little dramas the better you will be.

In so far as we can assume we have one life, it is far too precious for us to waste time licking our wounds when we could be recovering and getting on with embracing the wonders that are available for us to experience every day.

PERSONAL RESILIENCE

Resilience comes from the Latin word 'resilio' which means 'to jump back' and is used in everyday language to describe our ability to cope with and bounce back from adversity. Some people describe it as the ability to bend instead of breaking when under pressure or difficulty, or the ability to persevere and adapt when faced with challenges. The same abilities also help to make us more open, and willing, to take on new opportunities. In this way being resilient is more than just survival, it is also about letting go and learning to grow.

A resilient person is not only able to handle difficult experiences as they happen, they are also good at bouncing back quickly afterwards. The good news is that we can all develop our resilience by managing our thoughts, behaviours and actions.

RESEARCHING RESILIENCE

Over the past few decades, psychologists have discovered that the elements of natural resilience can be identified. From this knowledge, ways of helping those with low resilience can be developed. In a stressful, fast-changing world, boosting resilience in individuals and communities can help inoculate against depression and other mental illness, while boosting self-confidence, achievement levels and general productivity.

The American Psychological Association, which has studied resilience closely since the terrorist attacks of 9/11, defines it as the ability to adapt well in the face of adversity, trauma, tragedy, threats, and from sources of stress such as work pressures, health, family or relationship problems.

When we talk about resilience, most of us use the word fairly loosely. Often it's intended to mean the same as words like hardy, tough, irrepressible, stamina or even stick-ability.

Psychologists, however, use the word with much more precision.

William Frankenburg, one of the fathers of resilience research, pioneered an approach that builds on and strengthens resilient traits. Positive resilience theory rejects the idea that risk is something to be avoided. Instead, it focuses on those factors that promote well-being in individuals faced with adversity. Rather than take a defensive stance against risk, resilience theory takes the view that life, with all of its ups and downs, is there to embraced – and that coping with risk and bouncing back from adversity are positively good for us.

HOW IS YOUR BOUNCE ABILITY?

Do you have the 'bounce ability factor', the capacity to dust yourself off, stay calm and carry on? Or do you find bouncing back from adversity challenging and exhausting? Do you ever feel like just giving up?

You may well ask 'Why is it that some people thrive in the face of challenge and adversity, while others panic and withdraw into themselves? And why is it that some people manage to keep ahead whilst others just tread water, or slowly drown in the turbulent waters of life?'

Most people think that a combination of intelligence, long working hours and lots of experience allows people to thrive. In fact, it is those with resilience who cope best with challenges like constant change and upheaval, impending financial cutbacks, looming deadlines, arguments and incessant pressure.

The good news is that, although some people seem to be born with more resilience than others, those whose resilience is lower can learn how to boost their ability to cope, thrive and flourish when the going gets tough.

It takes practice and effort, but it is most certainly something worth working on if you want to get the best out of your life and cope better with everything that comes your way.

HOW TO BE MORE RESILIENT

Recently, I was in Cambodia doing some work with UNAKRT – the United Nations Assistance to the Khmer Rouge Trials. The trials began on the day I arrived, and I was working with some of the people who had been responsible for interviewing witnesses. They had spent a great deal of time listening to some of the atrocities that the Cambodian people had been subjected to.

We discussed at length the strength of the human spirit and how people react to adversity. It was fascinating to get different perspectives on what makes people more resilient than others and, indeed, the techniques that people use. From my own research, and these rather poignant conversations, it seems that there are some key behaviours that people possess that help them to jump back from even the most extreme hardship.

This is by no means a definitive list, but it is a great starting point.

Take emotional control

Some people internalize and withdraw when something difficult and challenging happens. Some people like to externalize and let the whole world know about it. Some people can be total drama queens and turn molehills into mountains. Being emotionally aware, and cultivating your ability to recognize how you can potentially react in certain situations, will help you to gain more self-control. It will also help you to be more considerate with regards to how your reactions can affect other people.

High emotion can be quite exhausting, so trying to balance and manage emotions during any ordeal will help you to focus your energy where it is best placed. People who have better emotional

self-awareness are more able empathize, and read and understand the emotions of others. This is important for resilience for
two reasons: first, it helps build relationships with others and then
this gives more social support.

Avoid the 'poor me' syndrome

When something difficult happens, there is a risk that we end up
feeling sorry for ourselves. It isn't very helpful and will often drive
us further away from where we really want to be. Some people,
however, seem to derive some sort of comfort from playing the
victim and asking the questions 'Why does this always happen to
me?' It strikes me that people who choose to adopt this attitude
(because it *is* a choice) have some kind of expectation that someone
else will come along and 'fix' their problem. Not only is this kind of
mentality self-centred, it is also very draining for other people.

Take responsibility

Taking responsibility for your circumstances and not looking for
ways to apportion blame enables you to seek out solutions. It is
by the far the most progressive and productive way to approach
any adversity. Often, you are more in control than you might think.
If you find yourself sitting in the passenger seat then you need
to get into the driving seat and navigate your own way through
whatever it is you are experiencing.

Be optimistic

Optimism is about being hopeful and believing that this time will
pass and there is the potential for things to improve. Realistic

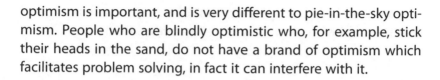

optimism is important, and is very different to pie-in-the-sky optimism. People who are blindly optimistic who, for example, stick their heads in the sand, do not have a brand of optimism which facilitates problem solving, in fact it can interfere with it.

Staying positive during dark periods can be difficult, but maintaining a hopeful outlook is important. Being an optimist does not mean ignoring the problem in order to focus on positive outcomes. It means understanding that setbacks are transient and that you have the skills and abilities to combat the challenges you face.

Be flexible

Flexibility is an essential part of resilience. By learning how to be more adaptable, you will be much better equipped to respond to adversity or any life crisis you experience. Resilient people often utilize these events as an opportunity to branch out in new directions. While some people may be crushed by abrupt changes, highly resilient individuals are able to adapt and thrive. When we accept that there is no such thing as forever, and that everything changes, we start to bend not break.

Believe in yourself

Research has demonstrated that self-esteem plays a very important role in coping with stress and recovering from difficult events. Remind yourself of your strengths and accomplishments. Keep a record of these – in a book or journal – to remind yourself what you are capable of achieving. Becoming more confident about your own ability to respond and deal with crisis is a great way to build resilience for the future. Challenges can be stepping stones or stumbling blocks. It's just a matter of how you view them and how much faith you have in yourself to overcome them.

Look after yourself

When you're stressed, it can be all too easy to neglect your own needs. Losing your appetite, overeating, not exercising, not getting enough sleep, drinking too much alcohol, not drinking enough water, driving yourself too hard, these are all common reactions to a crisis situation. Focus on building your self-nurturing skills, especially when you are troubled. Make time to relax and to embark on activities that you know make you feel better. Take time to invest in your well-being and you will boost your overall health and resilience and be fully ready to face life's challenges. Remember, at times like this you are more vulnerable and prone to illness, so make sure you indulge in a little tender loving care.

Learn to let go

A key part of resilience is the ability to let go. Some people carry so much personal baggage around with them which will certainly affect their ability to bounce.

There is a well-known Zen story, about two monks, which sums this up quite well.

A senior monk and a junior monk were traveling together. At one point, they came to a river with a strong current. As the monks were preparing to cross the river, they saw a very young and beautiful woman also attempting to cross. The young woman asked if they could help her.

The senior monk carried this woman on his shoulder, forded the river and let her down on the other bank. The junior monk was very upset, but said nothing.

As they continued on their journey, and senior monk noticed that his junior was suddenly silent and enquired 'Is something the matter, you seem very upset?'

The junior monk replied, 'As monks, we are not permitted to touch women, how could you then carry that woman on your shoulders?'

The senior monk replied, 'I left the woman a long time ago at the bank, however, you seem to be carrying her still.'

The older monk, his mind free, saw the situation, responded to it, and continued to be present to the next step after letting the woman down.

The younger monk was bound by ideas, held on to them for hours and, in doing so, missed the experiences of the next part of the journey. Mental attachment to an idea or an earlier experience blocks the full experience of the present – of the here and now. Baggage and attachments slow the mind, interfering with appropriate responses to the immediate situation.

In order to evaluate a situation requiring a decision, the mind must be open to all possibilities. Being anchored in the past can restrict our choices.

A great expression that I came across a few years ago is 'SUMO', which means 'shut up, move on'. I found this very useful because it is easy sometimes to get caught in the past, reliving situations and speculating on what we could have, would have, should have done. 'Shoulding' on ourselves is such a waste of time because we cannot wind the clocks back, and we cannot change the past. We can only positively learn from it and then let go.

Avoid catastrophizing

Catasrophizing is a form of distorted thinking which exaggerates the consequences of an action by thinking of it as a catastrophic event. Albert Ellis, the creator of Rational Emotive Behavior Therapy, referred to this as 'awfulizing'. Situations that are perceived as unwelcome or unpleasant get magnified in a person's mind in an awful way. You may well have experienced this yourself, or observed it in others. Highly anxious and stressed people are prime candidates for this way of thinking. A highly active imagination can trigger thought patterns that almost take on a life of their own and, before we know it, we have 'lived' the experience before it has actually happened. Some people can talk themselves into an emotionally charged state by thinking like this – and the danger is that it can become habitual. I have certainly met people in my life who, when presented with a challenging situation, are capable of creating monstrous scenarios of the potential outcomes. This may be useful if you are Stephen King and you can earn a fortune churning out horror fiction books. However, it's not helpful in the real world.

Develop your problem solving skills

Whenever you encounter a new challenge, make a quick list of some of the potential ways you could solve the problem. Experiment with different strategies and focus on developing a logical way to work through common problems. By practising your

problem-solving skills on a regular basis, you will be better prepared to cope when a serious challenge emerges. Self-efficacy is
the confidence you have in your ability to solve problems. This is
partly about knowing what your strengths and weaknesses are
and relying on your strengths to cope. It is also important to think
comprehensively about the problems you confront.

People who are more resilient are able to look at problems from
many perspectives and consider many factors. Just as a trapped or
cornered animal discovers an escape route within milliseconds,
your mind has subconscious drives, which intuitively search and
locate solutions. If you are stuck, it is because your mind has no
answer within its massive database. This is where creativity is a
good tool – a bit of lateral thinking can be useful.

Establish goals

Crisis situations are can be daunting and they can even seem
overwhelming and insurmountable. Resilient people are able to
view these situations in a realistic way, and then set reasonable
goals to deal with them. When you find yourself becoming overwhelmed by a situation, take a step back to simply assess what is
before you. Brainstorm possible solutions, and then break them
down into manageable steps.

There are lots of benefits to setting goals. First and foremost, they
help you to develop clarity, which is the first step to helping you
achieve what you want in life. Goals unlock your positive mind and
release energies and ideas for success and achievement. Without
goals, you simply drift and float on the currents of life. With goals,
you fly like an arrow, straight and true to your target. Setting goals
gives you direction, purpose and focus.

When you get clear about where you want to go, you set up steps and actions to get there. This helps you to break things into far more manageable chunks and to feel calmer and more in control. Goal setting also increases your efficiency because you are working on what is really important. Because you are focused your confidence increases. You will start to reap the benefits that a potentially traumatic situation can present and understand that there is an opportunity in every situation.

Develop a strong and supportive network

A strong network of supportive friends, family and work colleagues will act as a protective factor during times of crisis. It is important to have people you can confide in. Whilst simply talking about a situation with a friend or loved one will not necessarily make it go away, it will allow you to share your feelings, gain support, receive feedback and come up with possible solutions to your problems.

Listening to other people's experiences can be really useful too and, although we can't always learn from others' mistakes, there will certainly be some good advice out there if we can calm ourselves and listen attentively.

Some of the greatest learning that we experience can arise from the most painful and challenging situations. These situations help us to grow. They can strengthen us. One way that I look at it is that if we were totally happy, healthy, and content all the time, it is unlikely that we would think about our own personal growth.

Sometimes bad experiences can help us to take the time to look inside, to see who we really are, to learn how to feel compassion for others' pain and to keep an open mind regarding new and different beliefs. We can also learn how to stand up for ourselves and to discover ways we may never have explored before.

Problems are to the mind what exercise is to the muscles
– they toughen and make strong.

Norman Vincent Peale

So, even in your most challenging moment, remind yourself that
this time will pass and you will be stronger and more enlightened
and educated as a result. Learn the lesson and bounce back a little
bit stronger and a little bit better each time!

Bounce ability: top tips

✓ Take emotional control and manage your reaction to
adversity
✓ Take personal responsibility and avoid a victim
mentality
✓ Be optimistic and keep an open, flexible mind
✓ Believe in your ability to overcome adversity and bounce
back
✓ Look after your physical heath
✓ Learn to let go and avoid inflammatory internal
language
✓ Learn how to be more creative and better at problem
solving
✓ Set goals and break problems into digestible chunks
✓ Cultivate a supportive social network
✓ Learn from every experience and turn each problem into
an opportunity

Our greatest glory is not in never falling, but in rising
every time we fall.

Confucius

7

LIFELONG
LEARNING

I am still learning.

Michelangelo

*O*ne day, a teacher called Mr Sherrington told his young class to ask their parents for a family story with a moral at the end of it.

The next day in the classroom Andrew gave his example first.

'My dad is a farmer and we have chickens. One day we were taking lots of eggs to market in a basket on the front seat of the truck when we hit a great big bump in the road. The basket fell off the seat and all the eggs broke. The moral of the story is not to put all your eggs in one basket.'

'Very good', said Mr Sherrington 'Well done'.

Isobel put up her hand to go next. 'We are farmers too. We had twenty eggs waiting to hatch, but when they did we only got ten chicks. The moral of this story is not to count your chickens before they're hatched.'

'Very good', said Mr Sherrington again, pleased with the response so far.

Next it was little Fran's turn to tell her story: 'My dad told me this story about my great Aunt Paula. She was a flight engineer in the war and her plane got hit. She had to bail out over enemy territory and all she had was a bottle of whisky, a machine gun and a machete.'

'Go on', said Mr Sherrington, intrigued.

'Well, Great Aunt Paula apparently drank the whisky then found herself surrounded by a hundred enemy soldiers. She killed seventy of them with the machine gun until she ran out of bullets. Then she killed twenty more with the machete till the blade broke. And then she killed the last ten with her bare hands.'

'Good heavens', said the horrified Mr Sherrington, 'What did your father say was the moral of that very frightening story?'

'Stay away from Great Aunt Paula when she's been drinking.'

****

Certainly there is a lesson to be learned from everything you experience in life, and learning new things helps you to continue growing and keeps you engaged, motivated and happy.

Learning affects your well-being in lots of positive and exciting ways. It exposes you to new ideas and helps you to stay curious and engaged. It will also give you a sense of accomplishment and help boost your self-confidence and personal resilience.

There are so many ways to learn new things, whether it is learning a new sport or skill, joining a club, learning a new language or even just trying something you never thought you would be capable of. The beauty of learning new things is that it is not just about your own self-confidence and personal development, it also positively encourages others around you to try new things too.

I tend to think of learning as an essential exercise for the mind, just in the same way that our bodies need to stay active, we also need to work our minds, especially as we age. An alert and active mind ensures that you feed your most valuable asset. Keeping an open and curious mind will improve your sense of well-being and zest for life

THE BENEFITS OF LEARNING

Learning does not just mean studying for qualifications or to improve job opportunities. It can cover a whole range of mind-expanding and physical opportunities. Learning can develop new, update old, or build on current skills. Learning something new can open a multitude of doors for you. It can help you to earn more money, get a better job or do something you really enjoy. It can be a way to meet new people, share new experiences and reveal some of the hidden talents you didn't even know you possessed.

A challenged, stimulated mind may well be the key to a vibrant later life. As the baby boomers prepare to redefine their own retirement, research implies that staying active and keeping our brains constantly engaged may help stave off mental and physical ailments and diseases that we are susceptible to as we get older.

LEARNING AND INTELLIGENCE

Our approach to learning is very much dependent on what works for us, because every person is unique. Some people may self limit their potential to learn new things because they feel they lack intelligence. From my experience, academic qualifications have very little bearing on people's ability to learn and sometimes they are weighted far too heavily in the selection process for job roles.

Everybody is a genius. But if you judge a fish by its ability to climb a tree, it will live its whole life believing that it is stupid.

Albert Einstein

Interestingly enough, a theory of multiple intelligences was developed in 1983 by Dr. Howard Gardner, professor of education at Harvard University.

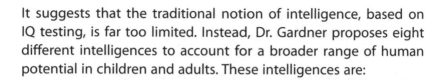

It suggests that the traditional notion of intelligence, based on IQ testing, is far too limited. Instead, Dr. Gardner proposes eight different intelligences to account for a broader range of human potential in children and adults. These intelligences are:

1 Linguistic intelligence – words, spoken or written

People with high verbal-linguistic intelligence display a facility with words and languages. They are typically good at reading, writing, telling stories and memorizing words along with dates. They tend to learn best by reading, taking notes, listening to lectures, and discussion and debate.

They are also frequently skilled at explaining, teaching and oration or persuasive speaking. Those with verbal-linguistic intelligence learn foreign languages very easily as they have high verbal memory and recall, and an ability to understand and manipulate syntax and structure. This intelligence is highest in writers, lawyers, philosophers, journalists, politicians, poets, and teachers.

2 Logical-mathematical intelligence – logic, abstractions, reasoning and numbers

It is often assumed that those with this intelligence naturally excel in mathematics, chess, computer programming and other logical or numerical activities.

A more accurate definition places emphasis on traditional mathematical ability and high reasoning capabilities, abstract patterns of recognition, scientific thinking and investigation, and the ability to perform complex calculations. It correlates strongly with traditional concepts of 'intelligence' or IQ. Many scientists, mathematicians, engineers, doctors and economists function on this level of intelligence.

3 Visual-spatial intelligence – vision and spatial judgement

People with strong visual-spatial intelligence are typically very good at visualizing, and mentally manipulating objects. Those with strong spatial intelligence are often proficient at solving puzzles. They have a strong visual memory and are often artistically inclined.

Those with visual-spatial intelligence also generally have a very good sense of direction and may also have very good hand–eye coordination, although this is normally seen as a characteristic of bodily-kinaesthetic intelligence. Careers that suit those with this intelligence include artists, engineers and architects.

4 Bodily-kinaesthetic intelligence – bodily movement

People who have this intelligence usually learn better by getting up and moving around, and are generally good at physical activities such as sports or dance. They may enjoy acting or performing and, in general, they are good at building and making things. They often learn best by doing something physically, rather than reading or hearing about it.

Those with strong bodily-kinaesthetic intelligence seem to use what might be termed 'muscle memory', and they remember things through their body such as verbal memory or images. Careers that suit those with this intelligence include football players, athletes, dancers, actors, surgeons, doctors, builders, and soldiers.

5 Musical intelligence – rhythm, music, and hearing

Those who have a high level of musical-rhythmic intelligence display greater sensitivity to sounds, rhythms, absolute pitch and music. They normally have good pitch and may be able to sing, play musical instruments and compose music.

Since there is a strong auditory component to this intelligence, careers that suit those with this intelligence include instrumentalists, singers, conductors, disc-jockeys, orators, writers and composers.

6 Interpersonal intelligence – interaction with others

People who have a high interpersonal intelligence tend to be extroverts, characterized by their sensitivity to others' moods, feelings, temperaments and motivations, and their ability to cooperate in order to work as part of a group.

They communicate effectively and empathize easily with others, and may be either leaders or followers. They typically learn best by working with others and often enjoy discussion and debate. Careers that suit those with this intelligence include politicians, teachers, managers and social workers.

7 Intrapersonal intelligence – introspective and self-reflective capacities

Those with strong intrapersonal intelligence are usually highly self-aware and capable of understanding their own emotions, goals and motivations. They often have an affinity for thought-based pursuits such as philosophy. They learn best when allowed to concentrate on the subject by themselves.

There is often a high level of perfectionism associated with this intelligence. Careers that suit those with this intelligence include philosophers, psychologists, theologians, writers and scientists.

8 Naturalist intelligence – nature, nurturing and relating information to one's natural surroundings

Those with it are said to have greater sensitivity to nature and their place within it, the ability to nurture and grow things, and greater ease in caring for, taming and interacting with animals. They may also be able to discern changes in the weather or similar fluctuations in their natural surroundings. Recognizing and classifying things are at the core of a naturalist.

They must connect a new experience with prior knowledge to truly learn something new. Naturalists learn best when the subject involves collecting and analyzing, or is closely related to something prominent in nature; they also don't enjoy learning unfamiliar or seemingly useless subjects with little or no connections to nature. It is advised that naturalistic learners would learn more through being outside or working in a kinaesthetic way. Careers that suit those with this intelligence include vets, environmentalists, scientists, gardeners and farmers.

Dr. Gardner believes that our schools and culture focus most of their attention on linguistic and logical-mathematical intelligence. We esteem the highly articulate or logical people of our culture. However, Dr Gardner says that we should also place equal attention to individuals who show gifts in the other intelligences: the artists, architects, musicians, naturalists, designers, dancers,

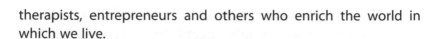

therapists, entrepreneurs and others who enrich the world in which we live.

LEARNING STYLES

It is also useful to understand that we are all different and we will learn in different ways. Knowing and understanding your learning style can make a big difference to how well you learn and at what speed. There are so many interesting models about learning; however, here is one of my favourite explanations of the different approaches to learning.

- **Auditory or Visual Learners.** This indicates the sensory mode you prefer when processing information. Auditory learners tend to learn more effectively through listening, while visual learners process information by seeing it in print or other visual modes including film, picture, or diagrams or videos when available.

- **Applied or Conceptual Learners.** This describes the types of learning tasks and learning situations you prefer and find most easy to handle. If you are an applied learner you prefer tasks that involve real objects and situations. Practical, real-life learning situations are ideal for you. If you are a conceptual learner, you prefer to work with language and ideas; practical applications are not necessary for understanding.

- **Spatial or Non-spatial Learners.** This reveals your ability to work with spatial relationships. Spatial learners are able to visualize or 'mentally see' how things work or how they are positioned in space. Their strengths may include drawing, assembling things, or repairing. Non-spatial learners lack skills in positioning things in space. Instead they tend to rely on verbal or language skills.

- **Social or Independent Learners.** This reveals your preferred level of interaction with other people in the learning process. If you are a social learner you prefer to work with others – both peers and instructors – closely and directly. You tend to be people-oriented and enjoy personal interaction. If you are an independent learner, you prefer to work and study alone. You tend to be self-directed or self-motivated, and often goal-oriented.

- **Creative or Pragmatic Learners.** This describes the approach you prefer to take toward learning tasks. Creative learners are imaginative and innovative through discovery or experimentation. They are comfortable taking risks and following hunches. Pragmatic learners are practical, logical and systematic. They seek order and are comfortable following rules.

LIFELONG LEARNING

Lifelong learning is the continued educational experience that we can embrace, perhaps through non-credit academic courses, travel, new hobbies, reading, listening to others, community service and volunteerism. It is an essential way to engage the brain fully, heighten physical activity, maintain healthy social relationships and to continue to grow and develop.

When you recognize the benefits gained from keeping your mind sharp you will realize that learning is like a health club for your mind. An active mind can stimulate physical activity and keep your spirits high. It's a fantastic all-round tool for better health. Lifelong learning helps fully develop natural abilities. Some of which might not be readily apparent. One advantage of retirement is that when you are no longer working full time, you will have even more opportunity to fully explore and develop these abilities.

Learning also opens the mind and promotes the free exchange of ideas and viewpoints. There is nothing like listening to, or taking part in, stimulating discussions to help us see the other side of an issue. That give and take opens our minds and brings us to a whole new level of enlightenment.

The more we discover about history, current events, politics or the culture of other countries, the more we want to learn. There is a big world out there just waiting to be explored. Travel is certainly a fabulous education and our drive and desire to learn more fuels itself and we keep going, constantly looking for more things to understand and explore.

Learning also helps us to put our lives in perspective and increases our understanding of the whys and the whats of previous successes and setbacks, helping us understand ourselves better, thus improving our self-awareness and understanding of what makes us happy. Lifelong learning also helps us adapt to change. The world is in a state of constant flux. Often, as we get older, we might feel like the proverbial 'old dog that can't learn new tricks'. That is simply not true, as learning enables us to keep up with society's changes – especially the technology which seems to accelerate at an extraordinary rate these days.

Learning can make the world a better place. Through the community service aspect of lifelong learning, older learners can give back to their communities and to the world. What we have learnt during our lifetime can be translated into real value for the improvement of society.

When we discover new things and explore new interests it can helps us make new friends and establish valuable relationships. No one enjoys loneliness. And through meeting new people, forging friendships and relationships with others we can enjoy a more active social life. Five years ago I set up a creative writing group in Cheltenham where I live called The Montpellier's Writing Group. I can honestly say this is one my proudest achievements and, through the talent within the group, I learn so much and feel so enriched as a result.

However we learn new things, whether it is through academic learning, educational adventure, travel or a renewed sense of volunteerism, we can expand our awareness, embrace self-fulfillment, and truly create an exciting multidimensional life. How good does that sound?

I have outlined here a few tips that can help you to learn better and more easily.

1 Understand how you learn

The best strategy for improving your learning efficiency is to recognize your learning habits and styles. As I have already outlined, there are a number of different theories about learning styles, which can all help you gain a better understanding of how you learn best. Gardner's theory of multiple intelligences – of eight different types of intelligence – can help reveal your individual strengths.

2 Multi learn

Focus on learning in more than one way. There are many different ways of learning. For example, instead of just listening to something which involves auditory learning, find a way to rehearse the information both verbally and visually. This might involve describing what you have learned to a friend, taking notes, visualizing it in your mind or making a collage of what you have learnt. By learning in more than one way, you're further cementing the knowledge in your mind. The more regions of the brain that store data about a subject, the more interconnection there is. This cross-referencing of data means you have learned, rather than just memorized.

3 Improve your memory

If our brains were computers, we'd simply add a chip to upgrade our memory. The human brain, however, is more complex than even the most advanced machine, so improving our memory isn't quite so easy.

A strong memory depends on the health and vitality of your brain. Whether you are a student, a working professional interested in doing all you can to stay mentally sharp, or someone looking to preserve and enhance the grey matter, there are lots of things you can do to improve your memory and mental performance.

Working on improving your memory can be a very useful skill to acquire. Basic tips such as improving focus, avoiding overloading yourself and structuring what you are attempting to learn is a good place to start. However, there are many more lessons from psychology that can dramatically improve your learning efficiency. Explore the different techniques that are available. This will take time and patience, but once these skills are learnt they can help save you lots of time in the long run.

4 Teach someone else

One of the best ways to learn something is to teach it to someone else. You can apply the same principle today by sharing your newly learned skills and knowledge with others. Start by translating the information into your own words. This process alone helps solidify new knowledge in your brain. Next, find a way to share what you've learned. Some ideas include: finding a willing pupil, writing an article or writing a blog post. Participating in group discussions can be useful too.

5 Put it into practice

Putting whatever new knowledge or skills or behaviour into practice is one of the best ways to improve learning. When you are trying to acquire a new skill or ability, focus on gaining practical experience. Create a plan that helps you to be able to do that. If it is a new sport or athletic skill, perform the activity on a regular basis. If you are learning a new language then practise speaking with another person. Whatever it is, do something with it. You might learn a lot of information about something but if you don't put it into practice then what is the point?

6 One thing at a time

Trying to multitask can make learning less effective. The danger is you lose significant amounts of time as you switch between multiple tasks and you lose even more time when the tasks became increasingly complex. By switching from one activity to another, you will learn more slowly, become less efficient and make more mistakes. A good way to approach this, if you have a lot of things that you are having to process, is to allocate yourself a predetermined amount of time to focus your attention on the task at hand. It is also good to try to complete tasks rather than leave too many things half done as this will create extra mind clutter and make you less able to focus.

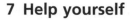

7 Help yourself

Learning is by no means a perfect process. There will be times when we forget the details of things that we have already learned, which can be frustrating. If you find yourself struggling to recall some information you are better off simply looking up the correct answer. The longer you spend trying to remember the answer, the more likely you will be to forget the answer again in the future.

We are very fortunate these days to be able to access the internet to find the answer to something. However, we also need to be selective because, as useful as the internet can be, it also has a lot of false information. My advice is: never rely on one source unless you are absolutely sure it is reliable. It's amazing how many 'false facts' fly about and how the truth can end up becoming distorted.

WHATEVER YOU DO, KEEP LEARNING!

One way to become a more effective learner is to keep learning. If you are learning a new language, it is important to keep practising the language, otherwise you will lose the momentum. This use-it-or-lose-it phenomenon involves a brain process known as 'pruning'. Certain pathways in the brain are maintained, while others are eliminated. If you want the new information you just learned to stay put, keep practising and rehearsing it.

It is also important that you enjoy the process and view learning as something that makes you feel good and not see it as a chore. Sadly, for those who had a poor experience at school or anywhere in education system, the term 'learning' may well not inspire. However, as you get older, you have the luxury of choosing more of the things you want to learn about. It opens the door to a whole host of opportunities and life benefits.

Every day we will learn something new, something that could make a profound difference to our lives, something that can make us feel really happy. We need to let any past negative experiences go, be open-minded, receptive and enthusiastic about learning new things every single day of our lives.

Lifelong learning: top tips

✓ Recognize the benefits of lifelong learning
✓ Understand your intelligences and your individual strengths
✓ Identify and understand your preferred learning style
✓ Learn in multiple ways to create variety and interest
✓ Work on improving your memory retention skills
✓ Teach someone else what you have learnt
✓ Put what you have learnt into practice as soon as you can
✓ Learn one thing at a time and remain focused
✓ Help yourself to learn by accessing reliable information sources
✓ Keep learning new things and enjoy the process

Anyone who stops learning is old, whether at twenty or eighty. Anyone who keeps learning stays young. The greatest thing in life is to keep your mind young.

Henry Ford

8

POSITIVE
RELATIONSHIPS

*The most important single ingredient in the formula of
success is knowing how to get along with people.*

Theodore Roosevelt

*M*r and Mrs Moody had been arguing all day and, as bedtime approached, neither was speaking to the other. It was not unusual for the pair to continue a war of silence for two or three days sometimes. However, on this occasion, Mr Moody was concerned.

He needed to be awake at 6 a.m. the next morning to catch an important business flight and, being a very heavy sleeper, he normally relied on Mrs Moody to wake him up. Cleverly, so he thought, when his wife was in the bathroom, he wrote on a piece of paper:

'Please wake me at 6 a.m. as I have an important flight to catch'. Mr Moody put the note on his wife's pillow, then turned over and went to sleep.

When he awoke the next morning and looked at the clock, it was 8 a.m.

Enraged that he had missed his flight, he was about to go in search of Mrs Moody to give her a piece of his mind, when he spotted a handwritten note on his bedside cabinet.

The note said: 'It's 6 a.m., time to get up, you don't want to miss your flight.'

****

You may not always get on with everyone all the time. You may, like the couple in the joke, end up in conflict with other people sometimes. However, endeavouring to cultivate positive and nurturing relationships in your life is important with regards to happiness.

The first step towards developing positive relationships is to be aware of the relationship you have with yourself. If you lack self-esteem, nurse a fragile ego, or have a negative attitude, it is far less likely that you will cultivate positive relationships. If you treat yourself as you would like others to treat you then that is a great starting point. It is also really important to treat other people as you would like to be treated, and an acute awareness of your behaviour and the effect you have on others is essential.

It is important that the people you invite into your life are there because you allow them to be. Sometimes it's good to take a good look at the people you surround yourself with – they will have a big influence on your life in so many ways.

RELATIONSHIPS

One of the most profound experiences that we can have in our lives is the connection we have with other human beings. People in supportive, loving relationships are more likely to feel healthy, happy and more satisfied with their lives and less likely to have mental or physical health problems or to do things that are bad for their health. People in supportive, loving relationships help each other practically as well as emotionally. Supportive partners share the good times and help each other through the tough ones.

A loving friendship can halve the troubles and double the joys and, by doing so, can make life's journey all the more enjoyable. So, when relationships work well, it can be a joyful and positive experience. However, as I am sure we have all experienced, when relationships break down and we find ourselves in a conflict situation or we simply do not connect with someone, it can be draining and disappointing and have a detrimental effect on our happiness.

The relationship that we have with ourselves is very important too. As I have already outlined in Chapter Two, you need to be your own best friend because if you don't like yourself how can you expect to cultivate a truly positive experience with yourself?

So, here are a few tips to help you to develop more positive and healthy relationships in your life.

ACCEPT AND CELEBRATE DIFFERENCES

One of the greatest things in life is that we are all different. However, one of the biggest challenges we experience in relationships is that we are all different. We can perceive the world in many ways. Certainly a stumbling block that we come across when we try to build relationships is a desire or an expectation that people will think like we do and, in this way, it is so much easier to create a rapport. We feel more comfortable when we feel that people 'get' us and can see our point of view. Life, however, would be very dull if we were all the same and, whilst we may find it initially easier, the novelty of sameness soon wears off.

So, whilst we may have different personalities, the first step to building relationships is to accept that we are all different. We will all have our own unique set of strengths and limitations. It is indeed better and more productive to spend time concentrating on improving our own limitations rather than criticizing those of others. It is far more positive to focus on peoples' strengths and accept that, for every strength they have, there is bound to be a perceived weakness.

Focusing on peoples' better qualities, and celebrating and feeding back their strengths, is a way to reinforce future positive behaviour. Many relationships break down because more time is spent eroding each other's self-esteem through negative criticism and trying to get each other to shrink fit into something or somebody that they are not. Also, it is important to recognize that sometimes, what we don't like in others is something that we don't like in ourselves!

LISTEN EFFECTIVELY

Listening is a hugely important skill in boosting another person's self-esteem, the silent form of flattery that makes people feel supported and valued. Listening and understanding what others communicate to us is the most important part of successful interaction and vice versa. When a person decides to communicate with another person, they do so to fulfil a need. The person wants something, feels discomfort, has feelings or thoughts about something. In deciding to communicate, the person selects the method or code which they believe will effectively deliver the message to the other person. The code used to send the message can be either verbal or nonverbal. When the other person receives the coded message, they go through the process of decoding or interpreting it into understanding and meaning. Effective communication exists between two people when the receiver interprets and understands the sender's message in the same way the sender intended it. Simple, you may think!

We were given two ears but only one mouth, because listening is twice as hard as talking.

There are three basic listening modes:

1 **Competitive or combative listening** happens when we are more interested in promoting our own point of view than in understanding or exploring someone else's view. We either listen for openings to take the floor, or for flaws or weak points we can attack. As we pretend to pay attention we are

impatiently waiting for an opening, or internally formulating our rebuttal and planning our devastating comeback that will destroy their argument and make us the victor.

2 **Passive or attentive listening** is when we are genuinely interested in hearing and understanding the other person's point of view. We are attentive and passively listen. We assume that we heard and understand correctly, but stay passive and do not verify it.

3 **Active or reflective listening** is the single most useful and important listening skill. In active listening, we are also genuinely interested in understanding what the other person is thinking, feeling, wanting or what the message means, and we are active in checking out our understanding before we respond with our own new message. We restate or paraphrase our understanding of their message and reflect it back to the sender for verification. This verification or feedback process is what distinguishes active listening and makes it effective.

Listening effectively is difficult, because people vary in their communication skills and in how clearly they express themselves, and often have different needs, wants and purposes for interacting. The different types of interaction or levels of communication also add to the difficulty.

As a listener, we attend to the level that we think is most important. Failing to recognize the level most relevant and important to the speaker can lead to crossed wires where the two people are not on the same wavelength. The purpose of the contact and the nature of our relationship with the person will usually determine what level or levels are appropriate and important for the particular interaction. If we don't address the appropriate elements, we will not be very effective, and can actually make the situation worse.

There is a real distinction between merely hearing the words and really listening for the message. When we listen effectively we understand what the person is thinking and/or feeling from the other person's own perspective. It is as if we were standing in the other person's shoes, seeing through their eyes and listening through their ears. Our own viewpoint may be different and we may not necessarily agree with the them but, as we listen, we understand from the other's perspective. To listen effectively, we must be actively involved in the communication process.

GIVE PEOPLE YOUR TIME

Giving time to people is also a huge gift. In a world where time is of the essence and we are trying to fit in more than one lifetime, we don't always have the time to give to our loved ones, friends and work colleagues. Technology has somewhat eroded our ability to build real rapport and we attempt to multitask by texting and talking at the same time!

Being present in the time you give to people is also very important, so that, when you are with someone, you are truly with someone and not dwelling In the past or worrying about the future. The connection we make with other people is the very touchstone of our existence and devoting time, energy and effort into developing and building relationships is one of the most valuable life skills.

DEVELOP YOUR COMMUNICATION SKILLS

Communication occurs when someone understands you, not just when you speak. One of the biggest dangers with communication is that we can work on the assumption that the other person has understood the message that we are trying to get across.

How many times have we experienced miscommunication through misunderstanding in the workplace that has either led to time wasting, deadlines not being met, or even conflict?

It is easy to see things from our own perspective, but much more difficult to look at them from another person's, especially when we all have different personalities, backgrounds, ideas and beliefs.

Poor communication in the workplace can lead to a culture of bitching, backstabbing and blame, which in turn can affect our stress levels, especially when we don't understand something or feel that we have been misled. When it works well it can have a very positive effect on morale – motivating individuals to come into work and do a great job.

The development of communication has provided us, in the last few decades, with a whole new range of media including email, instant messaging, the internet and mobile phones. All of these items undeniably enhance our communication. However, if mis-used, these gadgets can create issues and pose problems in the workplace. It is amazing how many people who sit five feet from each other will actually send each other email rather than speak. I know it is something that I have been guilty of.

The danger is that with more and more consumer-driven techno-logical toys being created, we are starting to shut out people in our everyday lives, and the same scenario is occurring in work environments throughout the world. If we really wanted, we now have the ability to go through an entire work day without uttering a word to a single colleague.

Clearly, if we continue to bypass face-to-face communication, our interpersonal skills will suffer as a result. Most human beings need personal interaction, are social creatures and thrive on cultivating and developing relationships with others. Many organizations encourage social interaction between employees and a sense of corporate community can affect staff morale, absenteeism and general overall performance.

Modern methods of communication can be a help and a hindrance. Thanks to the introduction of email, we no longer find memos in our trays, documents can be delivered more quickly and it's easier to relay information to colleagues simultaneously. While all this paper-saving is a dream come true for environmentalists, it doesn't do much to promote interpersonal communication.

Another risky factor about emails is that, if misread, they can easily be misinterpreted. Also, the other one poor communication habit is answering the phone and still continuing to read emails you can absolutely tell when that happens and it is clear that the person on the other end is not giving you their full attention. It is also poor manners. Just because that person is not in front of you, there is no excuse.

MANAGE MOBILE TECHNOLOGY

By now, pretty much everyone has a mobile phone and quite a few people have two or more. While they are a lifesaver in an emergency, and an effective tool for communication, they can also be a complete distraction when people exhibit a lack of mobile phone etiquette.

How many times have you watched people while they are in company playing with their phone, or sat in a meeting or on a train when somebody's mobile goes off? Or your colleagues are away from their desk and have forgotten to take their phones with them, thereby resulting in a cacophony of annoying phone rings, from Take That to Beethoven's Fifth?

I once spoke to someone who said that they felt undervalued by their manager. When I asked them why this was, I was horrified by her explanation. During her appraisal her manager's mobile phone went off. He then proceeded to postpone the rest of the performance review because something else had come up. Charming!

Too often I witness this poor use of mobile technology, which can really have a negative effective on the pursuit of building positive relationships. Being present when you are with someone is not only going to demonstrate that you value them, but it is also good manners!

LEARN TO GIVE AND TAKE FEEDBACK

Feedback, in my opinion, is the food of progress, and whilst it may not always taste great it can be very good for you. The ability to provide constructive feedback to others is really useful in terms of helping them to tap into their personal potential. It can help to forge really positive and mutually beneficial relationships. From your own personal perspective any feedback that you receive is free information and you have the choice entirely whether you want to take it on board or not. It is a great service with regards to helping you to tap into your blind spot and very useful in terms of getting a different perspective. The more open and receptive you are, the more useful it is.

By providing feedback to others you return the favour. However, some people find it very challenging to accept feedback, and get very uncomfortable around giving it, even when it is positive. Many of us get embarrassed by compliments, whereas if a remark is perceived as negative it can feel like criticism and cause us to get upset and defensive. Much of this is about how feedback is delivered. There are occasions where I have felt patronized when someone has delivered feedback. However, the key skill here is to see beyond the delivery technique and focus on the quality of the message. Remember, it's a gift; it's free information.

In acquiring the skill of being good at giving feedback, it is important first of all to ask yourself: 'will this feedback be useful, and can this person act upon it?' If the answer to both those questions is 'yes' then it is constructive.

I learnt years ago that a good approach is to tell someone what they did, explain the effect that it had, and help them to explore alternatives it if it is negative, or to keep on doing it if it is positive. It's important to get a balance of positive and negative. Sometimes, in the workplace or in relationships with loved ones, we spend a lot of time focusing on what someone isn't doing well, rather than celebrating the positives that will reinforce good behaviour and high self-esteem.

LEARN TO TRUST MORE

A long time ago, my brother and I had a very philosophical debate about what was most important in a relationship: love, trust or passion. I was a lot younger and more naive then and caught up in the heady rollercoaster of sensation seeking. I have grown to understand, however, that trust is hugely important in any relationship. Years later I bought my brother a photograph of a little girl, who was smiling and staring confidently at the camera with an elephant's foot just above her head. The strapline was: 'To trust is more important than love'. I believe that sentiment is true because no love will last without equal amounts of respect and trust.

To trust someone, however, takes courage. In my past I have been let down, as many people have. I have let people down, too.

However, we simply can't expect more from someone than we are capable of giving ourselves. The first step in developing trust is to learn to trust ourselves. Trusting ourselves to be able to cope when someone we love hurts us. Trusting ourselves to do the best we are capable of doing for most of the time. Trusting ourselves never to give up hope that tomorrow will be brighter, and that even if it's not we will handle it. We need to learn to trust that in the end all of our broken hearts, disappointments and hard won lessons will have a reason and play a purpose in our lives.

Once we trust ourselves we can be more open to trusting others. It's important to trust as much as you are personally comfortable with, and to accept that people may let you down from time to time. Sometimes you'll want to hide away and refuse to trust again but, if you trust yourself to always come out the other side of any situation both wiser and stronger, then the risk is not really that great. Don't give up on people. Most of them aren't trying to hurt you, and the few that are, usually don't matter that much in the scheme of your life for very long. So do yourself a favour: let them go so that you can keep an open heart and an open mind.

DEVELOP EMPATHY

A long time ago, I learnt a great saying that goes: 'People will forget what you said, people will forget what you did, but people will never forget how you made them feel.' Empathy and understanding build connections between people. Empathy is a state of perceiving and relating to another person's feelings and needs, without blaming, giving advice or trying to fix the situation. Empathy also means 'reading' another person's inner state and interpreting it in a way that will help the other person, offer support and develop mutual trust.

To truly empathize and understand another individual is an intuitive act where you give complete attention to someone else's experience and push aside your own issues. To be truly empathetic is to help another person feel secure enough to open up and share their experience. By being empathetic and understanding, you will make the other person feel that they are not entirely isolated in their predicament and provide them with a safe haven to recover and grow stronger knowing they have a compassionate supporter.

Empathy is different from sympathy. When someone is sympathetic, it also implies support; however, it is a feeling that is more fuelled by pity and an emotional distance is maintained from the other person's feelings. An empathetic and understanding approach is more about truly sensing or imagining the depth of another person's feelings. It implies feeling *with* a person, rather than feeling sorry *for* them.

Empathy is a translation of the German term *Einfühlung*, meaning 'to feel as one with'. It implies sharing the load, or 'walking a mile in someone else's shoes', in order to appropriately understand that person's perspective.

LET IT BE

When I was at school I had a 'best friend'. One day she decided to be someone else's 'best friend'. I was devastated as this was my first real experience of rejection. I took it as a great loss and felt very jealous towards her new 'best friend'.

One day I tried to explain this feeling to my father who told me that relationships are like sand in your hand. If you hold them too tight they will fall through your hands in the same way that sand will if you clench too hard. He told me that you cannot control the spirit of other people and, sometimes, you just have to let things be.

Years later, someone sent me a passage of writing called 'Reasons, Seasons and Life times', which suggests that people may enter your life in these three different ways. Sometimes it may be in order to teach you something or to help you in a very specific way. And because a person enters your life just for a season doesn't mean that it can't be a positive experience, which gives great pleasure. On the other hand, some people will enter your life and be with you throughout. However, the key message I took away was the importance of accepting each encounter for what it is, to take whatever transpires and appreciate the experience.

Every relationship we have can teach us something and, by building positive relationships with others, we will be happier, more fulfilled and feel more supported, supportive and connected.

Positive relationships: top tips

✓ Ensure that the relationship that you have with yourself is a positive one
✓ Accept and celebrate the fact that we are all different
✓ Actively listen to hear what other people have to say
✓ Give people time and 'be present' when you are with them
✓ Develop and work on your communication skills
✓ Manage mobile technology and be aware of its pitfalls
✓ Learn to give and take constructive feedback
✓ Open your heart and find the courage to trust
✓ Learn to be more understanding and empathetic
✓ Treat people as you would like to be treated yourself

Today we are faced with the preeminent fact that, if civilization is to survive, we must cultivate the science of human relationships . . . the ability of all peoples, of all kinds, to live together, in the same world, at peace.

Franklin D. Roosevelt

9

LIFE BALANCE

Wisdom is your perspective on life, your sense of balance, your understanding of how the various parts and principles apply and relate to each other.

Steven R. Covey

A *young man decided that he wanted to find out the secret to a happy life. After years of searching and not finding any satisfactory answers, he met a man who told him go to a cave, in which he would find a well.*

'Ask the well what is the truth', he was advised, 'and the well will reveal it to you'.

Having found the well, the young man asked the question. And from the depths of the well came the answer, "Go to the village across the road and there you shall find what you are seeking".

Full of hope and anticipation the man ran to the village to find only three rather uninteresting shops. One shop was selling pieces of metal, another sold wood, and thin wires were for sale in the third. Nothing and no one there seemed to have much to do with the revelation of happiness.

Disappointed, the man returned to the well to demand an explanation, but he was told only, 'You will understand in the future'. When the man protested, all he got in return were the echoes of his own shouts. Indignant for having been made a fool of – or so he thought at the time – the man continued his search.

As the years went by, the memory of his experience at the well gradually faded until one night, while he was walking in the moonlight, the sound of a violin caught his attention. It was being beautifully played with such skill.

Profoundly moved, the man felt drawn towards the player. He then became acutely aware of the violin itself. And then suddenly he exploded in a cry of joyous recognition.

The violin was made out of wires and pieces of metal and wood just like those he had once seen in the three shops and had thought it to be without any particular significance.

At last he understood the message of the well.

We have already been given everything we need, our task is to assemble and use it in the appropriate way. Nothing is meaningful so long as we perceive only separate fragments.

As soon as the fragments come together into a synthesis, a new entity emerges, which we would not have realized by considering the fragments separately.

****X***

This story is a great analogy with regards to living a happy and healthy life. I am a firm believer that in order to enjoy sustainable happiness we need to look at how we connect all the parts of our life. We need to take a holistic approach. This means finding balance and investing energy and care into our mind, body and soul.

When life is busy, or all your energy is focused on a something, it's all too easy to find yourself 'off balance', not paying enough attention to the important areas of your life.

Imagine life as a game in which you are juggling five balls in the air. You name them: work, family, health, friends and soul, and you are keeping all of these in the air. You will soon learn that work is a rubber ball. If you drop it, it will bounce back. The other four balls: family, health, friends and soul are made of glass. If you drop one of these, they will be irrevocably damaged or even shattered and they will never be the same again.

Too often in the fast paced lives that we lead we neglect the things that are the most important. Work takes over and your health suffers, or relationships start to disintegrate because you don't have the energy to nurture them. Sadly, some children grow up having a more in-depth relationship with the television or internet than they do with their parents.

LIFE BALANCE

'Work–life balance' is a phrase that has been bandied about since the 1970s. Personally, I think the term 'work–home balance' is a better description or just 'life balance'. Work–life balance tends to infer that we go to work and we have a life! The reality is that many of us spend more time at work than we do at home and more time with our work colleagues than we do with our friends and family so it is a huge part of our lives.

Work is fast becoming the way in which we define ourselves. It is now answering some of the traditional questions like 'Who am I?' and 'How do I find meaning and purpose in my life?' Work is no longer just about economics, it's about identity. About 50 years ago, people had many sources of identity: religion, class, nationality, political affiliation, family roots, geographical and cultural origins and more. Today, many of these, if not all, have been superseded by work.

The idea of work–home balance is further complicated by the fact that today's workforce is more culturally diverse, and made up of different generations, each with its own set of priorities. Additionally, businesses are in various stages of their own life cycles. Instead of looking for a generic, standardized concept of work–home balance, we need to understand that it is our own responsibility to make sure that we implement personal strategies that help us

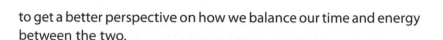

to get a better perspective on how we balance our time and energy between the two.

One important thing is the distinction between work and home – and to be aware of the negativities that we can potentially carry between the two. If we are not careful, it can become a bad habit that, at the end of a busy day, we offload to our partners all our moans and whinges about our time at work, thus infecting our home lives with the stress of work. A good habit to get into is spend time at the end of the day sharing achievements and successes and focusing on positive outcomes.

Work and home life are equally important, and the key to happiness is finding the right balance so you can get the best and the most out of both of them.

FINDING THAT BALANCE

Over the past 30 years, there has been a substantial increase in workload which is felt to be due, in part, to the use of information technology and to an intense, competitive work environment. Many experts forecasted that technology would eliminate most household chores and provide people with much more time to enjoy leisure activities. Unfortunately, many have decided to ignore this option, being egged on by a consumerist culture and a political agenda that has elevated the work ethic to unprecedented heights.

Life balance and personal happiness do not necessarily depend on earning more money and being successful at work or in business. Other things can have a much bigger impact on our well-being. Our age and 'life-stage' particularly affect what makes us happy and balanced, as does our personality, which stems from our genetic type, and our upbringing and life experiences.

Life balance is therefore changing and different. There is no single model that's right for everyone, and no single approach is right for anyone for their whole life. The search for happiness is further complicated because the factors which most affect our personal well-being are commonly ignored or given very low priority in work and training, and in the media too. In schools also, life balance and personal happiness are largely ignored, and rarely explored or recommended as worth pursuing.

Consequently, throughout our lives, we don't find it easy to consider properly the issues which actually determine our own personal life balance and happiness. Like most other things however, life balance and happiness can be managed and attained, if we know the components and the causes of our own well-being. Life balance can therefore be understood, planned and achieved, just like any other important ambition.

Once you've created space in your life for the things you love, it's just a matter of finding the right balance between them. You could have a life filled with all the things you love doing, but it could still be almost all work. It's better to have other things balancing out your life.

Variety is the spice of life so it pays to keep life interesting. Below are a few ideas to help you with balancing your life.

Find your own balance

Balance is an individual thing and everyone has to find their own equilibrium. It's up to you to prioritize, make adjustments and decide what you want and don't want. You can get advice, seek feedback and learn about what works for other people. However, ultimately what works for you can only be decided by you. You need to take personal responsibility for this. Don't tell yourself that you should be able to do something and, most importantly, don't listen to anyone else telling you what you should or should not be able to do!

Pay attention to your own needs and well-being. Stay in touch with how you are, physically and emotionally, and listen to your intuition. If you feel you're out of balance day in, day out, then you are! It's time to look at what's going on and re-evaluate.

Work out your priorities and prioritize effectively

Every time-management system tells you that you must prioritize your projects to make sure you are working on what is important instead of getting caught up in minor things. However, few systems explain precisely how to do this. How do you decide which task is really the most important at any given time? Is it the one that's most urgent, the one that will please someone else, earn you the most money or the one that will produce the greatest happiness?

You need to implement an intelligent method of prioritization, otherwise you will lack consistency and randomly bounce from one task to another. For prioritization to be effective and have meaning, it's imperative that you have a clear objective. Your personal objective may be a set of goals or a personal mission statement or purpose. The role of prioritization, then, is to help you achieve this result with as little effort as possible. The other consideration is the resources you have available. Your personal resources include time, money, your social network and your physical energy. Time is your most challenging resource because it cannot be replenished.

Learn how to time manage more successfully

Imagine if time was a bank account and, each morning, you were credited with 86,400 seconds. If, by the end of that day you hadn't spent any of the credits they would instantly be deducted from your account. What would you do?

Well, the chances are, I expect, that you would make every effort to spend them. It's amazing, isn't it, how much we take time for granted and then regret the moments we lost?

One of the biggest challenges that many people face is personal time management and the ability to prioritize. Let's face it, we all have our own quirky little habits that we have adopted; and I am sure we have all been guilty of putting ourselves and other people under unnecessary pressure by just not being as well-organized as we could.

It is important to respect other peoples' time and, if our own lack of personal organization or timekeeping disrupts others, to take responsibility and do something about it. Also, it is worth considering that, no matter how organized we may be, there are always only 24 hours in a day. Time doesn't change. All we can actually manage is ourselves, and what we do with the time that we have. Many of us are prey to time-wasters that steal time we could be using much more productively. It is so easy to go off-track or become distracted by something that is so much more interesting than the task in hand.

Procrastination is the ultimate thief of time, and putting off what we can do today is something many people are guilty of. It is actually far better to do the thing you least like doing first so that it doesn't hang over you making you feel gloomy at the prospect.

It is important to remember, the focus of time management is actually changing your behaviours, not changing time.

Greet the day

An early morning start is the best way to begin by having more time to get a better life balance. You give yourself that extra bit of time – and the more positive your day the better it will be. In the words of the Dalai Lama:

> Every day, think as you wake up, 'Today I am fortunate to have woken up, I am alive, I have a precious human life, I am not going to waste it. I am going to use all my energies to develop myself, to expand my heart out to others, to achieve enlightenment for the benefit of all beings, I am going to have kind thoughts towards others, I am not going to get angry or think badly about others, I am going to benefit others as much as I can.'

One tip that I have picked up is to 'refuse the snooze'. Let's face it, sometimes it is so tempting to press the snooze button and to snuggle up under the warmth and comfort of our duvets again and drift back into a semi-slumber. However, this is not the best way to start the day. Waking up and getting up to appreciate what the day has in store will bring you far more treasures.

There are many benefits to refusing the snooze: the early morning hours are so peaceful and so quiet, and a perfect time for setting the scene for your day ahead. You will also find that, by giving yourself some extra time, you won't find yourself rushing around playing catch-up, and any pressure you encounter during the day will be easier to manage.

Factor in thinking time

Thinking time is very important and, in the fast-paced world we live in, sometimes we don't feel we have time to schedule in thinking. However, if we are constantly running at everything we simply do not allow ourselves the opportunity to review and evaluate. We need to do that to determine what we are doing, how well it is going and if we are happy with it.

Often our lives become derailed from the track we set it on and, as a result, we don't realize where our lives are going until we really examine them. Or we can get so caught up in a routine that we don't realize we can change it. Regular self-reflection is the answer. Think about how your life is going, how you're spending your time, and decide whether you need to make changes. Then schedule time to make those changes or make them right away if you can.

Draw a line between home and work

If you're rushed and overloaded, what can happen is that while you're at work, you worry about things at home and when you're at home, you're preoccupied with work. It is really important for your emotional and physical well-being to be present wherever you are and not to focus on things that are not within your immediate control.

It is important to download the things on your mind before you leave work or home. Write a note in your diary, or on your PC, on your phone or on a piece of paper and list the things you need to do when you come back. Keep your mind focused on the fact that this is the end of that activity, workday or home task. Shut the diary, turn off your computer, save your message and draw the line. You cannot be in both places at the same time so choose to be in one only.

It is also important not to take your work stresses home. At the end of the day, if you are going to talk about work at home, focus on the things you have achieved rather than all the things that you haven't. You will feel a lot happier and positive if you choose to celebrate your successes and it will also be more conducive to a happy home environment.

Set yourself limits

Setting yourself personal limits is a useful thing to do at work or anything else that you tend to do too much. If you work ten to twelve hour days, for example, set a limit of eight hours per day, and stick to it.

If you are lucky enough to have a flexible schedule, you might consider working even less if you're trying to make more room. If you are self-disciplined and smart in your work approach you may be able to work out ways to make a four-day week work for you. What I've found is that if you set a limit you'll find a way to do the essential tasks within that limit. That might mean eliminating the non-essential tasks, cutting back on time-wasters such as casual internet surfing, and automating, delegating or outsourcing things you don't absolutely need to do yourself.

Those who demonstrate the propensity to be workaholics need to set boundaries for their own personal sanity – it is essential in order to get the balance right. All work and no play is dull!

Make time to spend with family and friends

Do you ever find yourself saying, 'I wish I had more time to spend with my family and friends'. So what stops you? What is so much more important than them? As with the ball juggling analogy that I used earlier, we need to nurture our relationships. With more marriages ending in divorce, more children practically having to self-rear, and people feeling more isolated and disconnected, it is important that we get the balance right here.

Plan romantic dates with your partner or dates with your friends or children or other family members. You don't have to call it a date, but just schedule time with them on a regular basis to do something together. It doesn't even have to cost a lot of money. It could be something simple like taking a walk in the park or playing a board game or cooking dinner together or sharing an interest or a hobby. These are the moments that we look back on in later life and cherish, not the ones where we stayed at work getting stressed and burnt out.

Develop new interests and hobbies

As we have already established, learning is very good for you and has numerous health benefits. You are never too old to learn something new and there is just so much out there that you could do. So many new pursuits can be very inexpensive or cost nothing at all. There are lots of free online learning websites, and a visit to the library could help you to learn a new language with some of the books and materials available. You could ask a family member to teach you something new, like how to play chess or poker.

One thing that I would highly recommend is that if you have a relatively sedate job then it's really important to balance your interest with something that is more active so that you get plenty of exercise. In the same way, if you have a very active job you may prefer something more relaxing. It is all about balance after all.

Feed your soul as well as your bank account

This is a critical balancing act that can be a challenge, too. We are actively encouraged by society to celebrate wealth and, sadly, many people see it as a benchmark of their success. How much someone earns is not, however, a good measurement from my own personal experience. Some of the most unhappy people I have ever met are also the most well-off materially. Some of the people I have met in places like Ethiopia, Thailand and Egypt, who appear to have literally nothing but the clothes on their backs and who live in very basic conditions, seem to be some of the happiest people I have come across.

What I have learnt is that real wealth is about attitude, not designer 'stuff'. It's about appreciating what you have and making the most of it. True we need to be realistic and we all have bills to pay. However, if we are working to the extent that we don't feel well enough or positive enough to enjoy it, what is the point?

Life most certainly is a balancing act and being able to juggle it effectively is something that we all need to endeavour to do if we really want to get the most and best out of it.

Life balance: top tips

✓ Find your own balance and what it means to you
✓ Work out your priorities and prioritize effectively
✓ Learn how to time manage more successfully
✓ Greet the day early and with a positive attitude
✓ Factor in thinking time to review and evaluate
✓ Draw a line between home and work
✓ Set yourself limits and create realistic parameters
✓ Make time to spend with your family and friends
✓ Develop new interests and hobbies
✓ Feed your soul as well as your bank account

*Happiness is not a matter of intensity but of balance
and order and rhythm and harmony.*

Thomas Merton

10

APPRECIATING LIFE

Happiness in itself is a kind of gratitude

Joseph Wood Krutch

A cosmic god had a horse. The horse was beautiful and had many good qualities. But the horse was dissatisfied and wanted to be more perfect in every way. In particular, it wanted to have unparalleled beauty.

One day the horse said to the cosmic god, 'Oh Lord, you have given me beauty. You have given me other good qualities. I am so grateful to you. But how I wish you could make me more perfect. I would be extremely, extremely grateful if you could make me more beautiful.'

The cosmic god said, 'I am more than ready to do what you ask. Tell me in what way do you want to be changed.'

The horse said, 'It seems to me that I am not well proportioned. My neck is too short. If you can make my neck a little longer, my upper body will be infinitely more beautiful. And if you can make my legs much longer and thinner, then I will look infinitely more perfect in my lower body.'

The cosmic god said, 'Amen!' Then immediately he turned the horse into a camel. The horse was so disheartened that it started to cry, 'O Lord, I wanted to become more beautiful. In what way is this more beautiful?'

The cosmic god said, 'This is exactly what you asked for. You have become a camel.'

The horse cried, 'Oh no, I do not want to become a camel I want to remain a horse. As a horse, everybody appreciated my good qualities. Nobody will appreciate me as a camel.'

The cosmic god said, 'Never try to achieve or receive more than I have given you. If you lead a life that you don't appreciate then at every moment you will want more and more. Each thing in my creation has

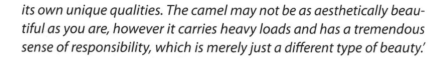

its own unique qualities. The camel may not be as aesthetically beautiful as you are, however it carries heavy loads and has a tremendous sense of responsibility, which is merely just a different type of beauty.'

****

A very wise person once told me 'Beauty is not found in a facial mole, true beauty is reflected from your soul.'

I suppose that is a lesson to us all, especially with so much media focus being on how someone looks. We can get so caught up in the pursuit of so-called 'betterment' that we don't stop and appreciate what we have and be grateful for it. The distance between reality and expectation is a good barometer of happiness and, if we live a life full of expectation, we can miss what is right in front of us.

A few months ago, I was presenting at a large conference for a team of sales people. I was speaking about the concept of taking time each day to consider what we are grateful for. I explained how scientific evidence, that gratitude improves health, comes from research accumulated by Robert Emmons, professor of psychology at the University of California. Through extensive research, Dr Emmons has found that gratitude can make you up to 25 per cent happier.

I introduced the concept of vitamin G (vitamin gratitude – although vitamin G used to be the old term for Riboflavin, so try not to get confused, even though both are very good for you). I suggested to everyone that they take a gratitude stone in their hands each morning or evening and just spend a few minutes reflecting on all the things in their lives that they are grateful for. I then offered a range of gratitude stones that I had brought along to everyone in the audience.

A participant on the front row caught my attention when I saw him mouth to the colleague sitting next to him, 'What a load of b******s!' Clearly, he wasn't taken with the concept, so I suggested to him that it was his choice to come and take a stone and, if he didn't want to, then that was perfectly OK; different things work for different people. Rather begrudgingly, however, he came up and took his stone.

About two weeks later, he telephoned me. He introduced himself and said: 'You probably don't remember me'. *Oh yes, I do!* I thought.

He explained politely how he had enjoyed my presentation, although that he hadn't really bought into the gratitude concept. He wanted to tell me, however, what had happened to him when he got home. He had lent his brand new car to his wife for the day, and when she had greeted him, somewhat pale-faced and anxious at the front door, she announced that she had two pieces of bad news.

The first piece of news was that she had reversed the car out of the drive and driven too close to the gate, scratching all the paintwork along the right-hand door. As he prepared to rant she dropped the second bombshell: their youngest son had been suspended from his very expensive boarding school. It transpired that the son had a general, bad attitude and consistently didn't deliver work projects on time. His father explained to me that he had been furious, especially considering that he worked ridiculous and gruelling hours to keep his family comfortable.

He had gone upstairs in a very bad mood and as he was getting undressed, he came across his stone. Feeling totally fed up, he had sat on his bed and seriously questioned the concept of gratitude.

He then explained to me that it had been one of the most emphatic moments for him, because two things had occurred to him immediately that he could be grateful for. The first was that even though his wife had scratched the car he was struck by the thought: *So what? At least she hasn't been hurt.* The second was that, despite the fact that his son was going through a challenging adolescent phase, at least he wasn't on drugs like some of his friends' children – which was a far worse situation.

He said that he had called me to share this epiphany with me, as he wanted me to know that a daily dose of vitamin G *does* work and now he keeps his stone on his desk and calls him Rocky!

I really must now credit this man for providing me with a great tale to tell when I talk about gratitude.

WHAT IS GRATITUDE?

The word 'gratitude' comes from the Latin word 'gracia', which means grace. Rather than living a life filled with stress, anxiety, and striving, gratitude gently teaches us the truth that all life is a gift to be received and enjoyed. I am sure we can all think of times in our lives when we've expressed heartfelt thanks and realized how positive it has made us feel. Being grateful has one of the best feel-good factors, and scientific research has indicated that it can make us happier and healthier, too.

Gratitude is an almost universal concept amongst cultures throughout the world. Being grateful has a number of other benefits, too. Feelings of gratitude are associated with less frequent negative emotions and can promote more positive emotions, such as feeling energized, alert, and enthusiastic. You can even experience pleasant muscle relaxation when recalling situations in which you were grateful. It is apparent that the act of giving thanks can have a remarkable impact on a person's well-being, and the best thing is that we can tap into this amazing resource any time we like!

An appreciative mindset can have a very powerful effect on the way we perceive our reality and, ultimately, the way we live our lives. By cultivating an attitude of gratitude, we can seek out and attract more positive things into our life to be grateful for.

The important thing about having an attitude of gratitude, however, is the quality of the feeling that accompanies it.

THE BENEFITS OF GRATITUDE

The study of gratitude within the field of psychology only began around the year 2000, possibly because psychology has tradition-ally been more focused on understanding distress than under-standing positivity. However, with the advent of the Positive Psychology Movement, gratitude has become a mainstream focus of research.

The main conclusions that have been drawn so far are that grateful people report higher levels of positive emotions, life satisfaction, vitality, optimism and lower levels of depression and stress. The disposition toward gratitude appears to enhance the feel-good factor. Grateful people, however, do not deny or ignore the nega-tive aspects of life; they simply focus on the potentially positive outcomes that can be manifested. They seek to turn problems into opportunities – creating *probortunities*!

People with a strong disposition toward gratitude have the capac-ity to be more empathic, and find it easier to take the perspective of others. They are rated as more generous and more helpful by people in their social networks.

Grateful people are more likely to acknowledge a belief in the interconnectedness of all life and a commitment to and responsibility for others. Gratitude does not necessarily require religious faith. However, faith and belief in something enhances the ability to be appreciative.

It also appears that grateful individuals place less importance on material goods; they are less likely to judge their own and others' success in terms of possessions accumulated; they are less envious of others and are more likely to share their possessions with others.

In a comparative study, those who kept gratitude journals on a weekly basis exercised more regularly, reported fewer negative physical symptoms, felt better about their lives as a whole, and were more optimistic about the upcoming week compared to those who recorded neutral life events.

A related benefit was also observed with regards to personal goal achievement. Participants who kept gratitude lists were more likely to have made progress toward important personal goals over a two-month period compared to subjects under other experimental conditions.

A daily gratitude intervention with young adults resulted in higher reported levels of the positive states of alertness, enthusiasm, determination, attentiveness and energy.

Participants in the daily gratitude condition were also more likely to report having helped someone with a personal problem or having offered emotional support to another person.

Research has also identified that children who practise grateful thinking have more positive attitudes toward school and their families.

Gratitude plays a key role in positive illness management and in a sample of adults with neuromuscular disease, a 21-day gratitude intervention resulted in greater amounts of high-energy positive moods, a greater sense of feeling connected to others, more optimism about their lives, and better sleep duration and quality.

Studies also provide evidence that a positive, appreciative attitude enhances the body's healing system and general health by helping it to produce more immune-boosting endorphins. When you hold feelings of thankfulness for at least 15 to 20 seconds, beneficial physiological changes take place in your body. Levels of the stress hormones cortisol and norepinephrine decrease, producing a cascade of beneficial metabolic changes. Coronary arteries relax and increase the blood supply to your heart. Your breathing becomes deeper, raising the oxygen level of your tissues.

GRATITUDE AND HAPPINESS

Gratitude has been the 'forgotten factor' in happiness research, and scientists are latecomers to the concept of gratitude. Religions and philosophies have long embraced gratitude as an indispensable manifestation of virtue and an integral component of health, wholeness and well-being. Through conducting highly focused studies on the nature of gratitude, its causes, and its consequences, scientists now hope to shed important scientific light on this important concept.

Gratitude is about appreciating and being thankful for what you have. The important thing about having an attitude of gratitude is the quality of the feeling that accompanies it.

Living with an attitude of gratitude can mean different things to different people, depending on your background and experiences in life. It can carry with it either good or not-so-good feelings. The kind of gratitude that the self-improvement gurus are recommending is obviously the good-feeling kind. This is the kind that is connected with a positive kind of gratitude attitude.

Gratitude is not just about saying 'thank you'. It is also about living in a state of thankfulness. It is about truly appreciating the people, experiences and circumstances that create an existence that is unique to you. Gratitude is a state of being which, when cultivated properly, projects itself from an individual out unto the world. It is not a reflective force; rather it generates its own source of energy from within. It is the internal combustion engine that powers our desire to help one another. Without gratitude, the seeds of hope and appreciation are never sown, and in their place the weeds of selfishness and self-pity are allowed take root. Gratitude, as the famous Roman orator Cicero said, is the parent of all other virtues. If you're looking for a good place to start improving your life, it would be to begin by expressing those things for which you are grateful.

So, I have a question for you. Do you have an attitude of gratitude? Are you thankful for each and every thing that you have in your life right now, or are you walking around complaining about what you are lacking?

Here are some useful tips to help you cultivate an attitude of gratitude and appreciate life more.

1 Decide to be grateful

It is entirely your choice whether you want to become a grateful person. If you decide to be a grateful person, then choose to be one. No matter what happens to you, it is still up to you to decide how you want to respond. When something happens to you – good or bad – learn to say thank you to each experience. Some may be wonderful and bring you immense joy; some may hurt you. However, they will make you stronger with the lesson you learn from them.

2 Wake up with an attitude of gratitude

You can train your mind to focus on anything you like. When you wake up, you immediately begin to consciously programme your subconscious mind on how your day will be. If you tell yourself that you are going to have a bad/stressful day, then you will, because your subconscious mind will believe anything your conscious mind tells it. Turn any negative thought around and discipline yourself to start every day with a positive and appreciative thought. This positive conditioning will set you up to have more positive and happy days.

3 Take a daily dose of vitamin G

I mentioned, when I was telling you the story about the sales director and the gratitude stone, that I called this vitamin G (Vitamin Gratitude). It can be anything really that you do each day that reminds you to focus on appreciation. A great way to do this is to have a gratitude stone by your bedside table or by your toothpaste, and remember to take it in your hand each morning and reflect upon what you are grateful for. Do this every day for a month and it will become embedded as a new habit and you will start to notice how good it makes you feel. I have delivered this concept now to thousands of people.

4 Keep a gratitude journal

Take vitamin G one step further and write about the good things that happen in your life in a journal, especially those which make you feel really happy. This is great to do before you go to bed at night, especially if you can't sleep. If you are feeling anxious or depressed, or you are worrying about something, it is a great way to help you to focus and train your wandering mind onto a more focused activity. When life looks dark and a bit gloomy, and it's difficult for you to be grateful, open and read your journal to remind yourself about the good things. Dwelling on the happy, positive stuff will help you to realize how wonderful life can be and will be again.

5 Create a gratitude list

This is slightly different to a journal. This is more about reminding yourself about some of the things in life that you can be grateful for and to remind yourself what is out there and how it makes you feel. You may want to start with listing what you are grateful about your life. Here are a few examples.

- Time, for a system to organize yourself and keep track of activities.

- Your job, for giving you a source of living and purpose.

- Mistakes, for helping you to improve and become a better person.

- Pain, for helping you to mature and become a stronger person.

- Laughter, for serenading your life with joy and happiness.

- Love, for letting you feel what it means to truly be alive.

- Life's challenges, for helping you grow and become who you are.

- Life, for giving you the chance to experience all that you are experiencing and will experience in time to come.

Every time you think of something you are grateful for, write it down.

6 Focus on giving

You will be grateful if your mind focuses on what you *have*, rather than what you *don't have*. By *giving*, your mind will focus on what you have (you can't give something you don't have, can you?), rather than what you don't have. Most people focus on *receiving*, which makes their mind focus on what they *don't* have. This is why it's difficult for them to be appreciative.

It is important to get the balance right in life, and giving can have a very positive effect on our own well-being. We live in a world where there seems to be a lot of the 'me, me, me' mentality, and 'I, I, I' attitude – think iPhones and iPads. There seems to be a sub-liminal message, reinforced by the media, that this self-centred approach is acceptable. However, sharing and giving to others is about being kind and compassionate, and giving makes you feel good too.

7 Get into the habit of saying 'thank you'

Do you always remember to say thank you? Are there times you forget because you are too busy? Perhaps when someone has sent you a gift and you haven't let them know how much you appreciated it. Perhaps, when you have been to dinner at someone's house, the next day you forget to let them know how much you enjoyed it. Even the routine things that your family or partner does, do you take it in your stride without acknowledgement? No one likes being taking for granted, so make sure that saying *thank you* is part of the daily fabric of your life.

Also make sure that saying thank you isn't a chore in your mind. Heartfelt, sincere thanks is not an obligation, it is a tangible sign of gratitude. When you say thank you to someone, look them in the eye and mean it! A small gesture like that could make all the difference to someone. Their day will glow a little brighter for being acknowledged and appreciated.

A nice thing to do at the end of each day is write down in your journal who you want to remember to thank for something that they have done that day and remind yourself to let them know how it made you feel if you haven't had chance to thank them already.

8 Highlight the best bits of your day

Getting into the habit of focusing on the best bits of your day is not only good fun, it is also a very uplifting thing to do. This is something you can do with your partner, family and friends. At the end of the day or perhaps over dinner with your children get everyone to take it in turns sharing the three best things that have happened to them and how it made them feel and why it made them feel good. This positive reinforcement exercise will help people to focus on the positives and diffuses and dilutes some of the negatives that may have occurred.

It can be a great tonic after a tiring day, when things haven't gone as well as you would have liked, to hear about other people's joys. It's not just therapy, it's entertainment!

Highlighting three things that make you happy is a wonderful way to summarize your day.

Appreciating your life is something that can bring a whole host of health benefits. People who have an attitude of gratitude are much more fun and positive to be around. Every day, in every way, we will always have something to be grateful for.

Count your blessings one by one and savour and appreciate each one.

Appreciating life: top tips

✓ Learn to appreciate what you have and make the most and best of it
✓ Understand the benefits to your overall well-being of being grateful
✓ Make the decision to be grateful and appreciate life
✓ Wake up with an attitude of gratitude and condition your mind

✓ Take a daily dose of vitamin G and focus on appreciation
✓ Keep a gratitude journal and write in it every day
✓ Create a gratitude list to reflect upon
✓ Focus on giving to others and sharing
✓ Get into the habit of saying 'thank you'
✓ Highlights the three best things that happen to you each day

He is a wise man who does not grieve for the things which he has not, but rejoices for those which he has.

Epictetus

11

CULTIVATING KINDNESS

My religion is very simple. My religion is kindness.

Dalai Lama

One day a man called Charles was sitting by a river, watching a scorpion floundering around in the water. He decided to save it by stretching out his finger, but the scorpion stung him. Charles still tried to get the scorpion out of the water, but the scorpion stung him again.

Another man nearby told him to stop trying to save the scorpion that kept stinging him.

Charles continued to help the insect and said: 'It is the nature of the scorpion to sting. It is my nature to love. Why should I give up my nature to love just because it is the nature of the scorpion to sting?'

****

The message here is to not give up your loving nature and your kindness even if other people around sting you. It is inevitable that people will do that, sometimes with malice and intention other times without even being aware that they have. I have always learnt that when people are not very nice to you be nice to them, not because they are nice, because you are.

A loving and compassionate heart is a far more constructive way to deal with something or someone than to feel bitter and resentful. Any negative emotion that we cultivate can be damaging, a focus on kindness will bring you far more peace and happiness.

EMPATHY, COMPASSION AND KINDNESS

I had a very interesting time during the research for this book, exploring the difference between empathy, compassion and kindness. It was fascinating discovering other peoples' understanding and definitions of the three.

The general consensus was that empathy was about having some understanding and identification with how any person is feeling about something that is happening. The metaphor of 'being able to put yourself in someone else's shoes' is often used to describe this. Empathy can be associated with any emotion or experience someone is feeling. You can empathize with someone about a joyous experience like falling in love, becoming a parent, discovering a new hobby or getting a great new job. It doesn't have to be a sad experience. It is the ability to relate to the whole spectrum.

Compassion is about having a deep awareness of the suffering of another person, coupled with the wish to relieve it. Compassion is also a virtue and the cornerstone of humanism. It is the general desire to want to help other people to feel better and happier.

Kindness, on the other hand, is about taking action. It is about *doing* something and, in many ways, is the most useful approach if you really want to help others actively. I really do believe, though, that it is important to cultivate an ability in all three behaviours in order to be able to take a rounded approach to happiness. There are occasions when people, with all the best will in the world, try to be kind; yet what they do is not appreciated and, in some cases, really not wanted. In order to know what will benefit someone else we need to have an understanding of their needs. Kindness is not just about doing something for someone when they are in a bad way, it is about cultivating a kind heart in your approach to everything.

We don't just do something for someone because they feel bad. We need to get the balance and it is great to do something for someone because, whilst they may well be happy, we can help them feel happier.

It's a bit like when you are in relationship and you stop making the effort to do nice things for your partner. All the special effort you made in the honeymoon period starts to become a distant memory. Relationships are like flowers and they need watering and nurturing to keep the romance alive. Thoughtful acts of kindness are a wonderful way to show that you still care.

Kindness also needs to be understood from different perspectives. What you might consider an act of kindness could be perceived by somebody else as sticking your nose into something that doesn't concern you. I certainly know on occasions I have been rebuffed and heard myself saying 'I was only trying to be kind'. So, if your intended kindness is directed at people, a good understanding of their feelings and being able to be understand the first is a good place to start.

UNDERSTANDING EMPATHY

Empathy is the emotional process that builds connections between people. It is a state of perceiving and relating to another person's feelings and needs, without blaming, giving advice or trying to fix the situation. Empathy also means 'reading' another person's inner state and interpreting it in a way that will help them – by offering support and developing mutual trust.

To truly empathize and understand another individual is an intuitive act where you give complete attention to someone else's experience and push aside your own issues. To be truly empathetic is to help another person feel secure enough to open up and share their experience. By being empathetic and understanding, you will make the other person feel that they are not entirely isolated in their predicament and provide them with a safe haven to recover and grow stronger knowing they have a compassionate supporter.

Empathy is different from sympathy. When someone is sympathetic, it also implies support; however, it is a feeling that is more fuelled by pity, where an emotional distance is maintained from the other person's feelings. An empathetic and understanding approach is more about truly sensing or imagining the depth of another person's feelings. It implies feeling *with* a person, rather than feeling sorry *for* them.

Empathy is a translation of the German term *Einfühlung*, meaning 'to feel as one with'. It implies sharing the load, or 'walking a mile in someone else's shoes', in order to appropriately understand that person's perspective.

Having a rich capacity for empathy and understanding is not only a great life skill, it is also a wonderful quality if it is used in the right way. It is an ability that can be used for good, or for evil. Once you understand someone you can use that understanding to help them, to heal them, to hurt them or to destroy them. If you reject the skill of empathy, you reject the ability to really understand your fellow humans as well as you could. In war, a lack of empathy can lead to defeat, in justice it can lead to injustice and, in relationships, it can kill love.

> *If there is any one secret of success, it lies in the ability to get the other person's point of view and see things from his angle as well as your own.*

Henry Ford

How to cultivate empathy

To increase your empathy, you need to start with yourself. Pay close attention to your emotional state and what gives rise to positive and negative emotions. Use this as a basis upon which to understand people's emotional responses.

We are very lucky in the so-called developed world that we have more opportunity to mix cross culturally and learn more about people from a wide range of backgrounds. Get to know people from all ages, ethnicities, sexual orientations, socio-economic backgrounds and levels of physical ability. The more types of people you get to know, the more experiences you will have to draw on as you try to increase your empathy.

Fostering empathy in those around you is a good thing to do and looking for similarities between yourself and others is interesting. When we focus on differences between ourselves and other people, it's much more difficult to understand others.

It is useful as well to practise taking on another's perspective. Educate and condition your mind to be open to the perspectives of others and immerse yourself in them. Not only will this improve your ability to be more empathetic, it will help you to grow.

UNDERSTANDING COMPASSION

The American monk, Bhikkhu Bodhi, states that compassion supplies the complement to loving-kindness. But whereas loving-kindness has the characteristic of wishing for the happiness and welfare of others, compassion has the characteristic of wishing that others be free from suffering, a wish to be extended without limits to all living beings.

Feeling and demonstrating compassion towards others is more than a sign of a healthy and positive worldview. It can benefit you both mentally and physically. Research has demonstrated that people who are more compassionate not only have lower blood pressure and cortisol levels, but are also more receptive to social support. So, in fact, looking outside of one's self actually benefits the self and, by fostering an attitude of compassion toward others, may be a way to improve your own sensitivity to stress.

The value of compassion cannot be over-emphasized.
Anyone can criticize. It takes a true believer to be
compassionate. No greater burden can be borne by an
individual than to know no one cares or understands.

Arthur H. Stainback

So, one of the main benefits of compassion is that it helps you to be more happy, and helps others around you to be more happy. If we agree that it is a common aim of each of us to strive to be happy, then compassion is one of the main tools for achieving that happiness. I would most certainly suggest, then, the importance of cultivating compassion in our lives and making sure that we practise it every single day. A compassionate heart is a healthy and happy heart.

As Albert Einstein observed, 'A human being is a part of the whole called by us universe, a part limited in time and space. He experiences himself, his thoughts and feeling as something separated from the rest, a kind of optical delusion of his consciousness. This delusion is a kind of prison for us, restricting us to our personal desires and to affection for a few persons nearest to us. Our task must be to free ourselves from this prison by widening our circle of compassion to embrace all living creatures and the whole of nature in its beauty.'

How to cultivate compassion

It would be really nice to be able to think that we can be compassionate in every situation, but sometimes, if we are having a bad day or someone isn't being very nice to us, it can be challenging. Compassion takes practice and, like anything, will take some effort on your part.

We need also to examine our approach sometimes – when another person is suffering we need to be careful that we don't end up getting so absorbed in feeling compassion for others that we lose a sense of our own well-being. Compassion for oneself, therefore, is a really good place to start.

You also need to be aware that sometimes we need to be cruel to be kind, being overly compassionate can mean that people who choose the victim mentality will prey on your generosity of spirit to feed their self-pity without even knowing it.

One way to practise compassion is to imagine the suffering of a human being you've met recently. Now, imagine that you are the one going through the suffering. Reflect on how much you would like that suffering to end. Reflect on how happy you would be if another person desired your suffering to end, and acted upon it. Open your heart to that person and, if you feel even a little that you'd want their suffering to end, reflect on that feeling. That's the feeling that you want to develop. With constant practice, that feeling can be grown and nurtured.

The way to progress this feeling is to imagine again the suffering of someone you know or met recently. Imagine again that you are that person, and are going through that suffering. Now imagine that another human being would like your suffering to end. What would you like for that person to do to end your suffering? Now reverse roles: you are the person who desires for the other person's suffering to end. Imagine that you do something to help ease the suffering, or end it completely. Once you get good at this stage, practise doing something small each day to help end the suffering of others, even in a tiny way like a smile, a kind word, an errand or chore or just talking to someone. Practise doing something kind to help ease the suffering of others.

The real test of compassion, however, is the desire to want to ease the suffering of those who mistreat us. One time, I became very sensitive and upset about something that someone had said to me that wasn't very nice. My friend Paul, who has been a great inspiration to me, asked me to imagine a time when I had felt happy, really really happy. He asked me how it made me feel towards other people. I responded by saying that it made me want to hug everyone and say complimentary things to them. Then I realized that when we are happy we very rarely hurt others.

Now, when someone isn't very nice to me, I try to remain calm and detached, and reflect on the person who has mistreated me. I try to imagine the background of that person; try to imagine what that person was taught as a child; try to imagine the day or week that person has been going through, and what kind of bad things have happened to them; try to imagine the mood and state of mind they are in, and the suffering that person must have been going through to mistreat me in that way. From this, I can understand that their action is not about me, but about what they are going through.

When someone isn't nice to you, remember you have a choice. You can choose to feel resentful or bitter, or you can treat that person with compassion in the hope that they will feel happier. They, in turn, will perhaps reflect on the way that you responded and, as a result, it may well influence their behaviour to others in future. You will also have spent time focusing on positive emotions and will be happier that you were able to do this.

UNDERSTANDING KINDNESS

When we see someone do something kind or thoughtful, or we are on the receiving end of kindness, it inspires us to be kinder ourselves. In this way, kindness spreads from one person to the next, influencing the behaviour of people who never witnessed the original act of kindness. It is the glue that connects people and is the key to creating a happier world.

Sometimes I think, wouldn't it be wonderful to live in a kind world? A place where everyone said nice things, doors were always held open, there was no spite and bullying and peace reigned supreme. However, in the real world, we have to be prepared for the fact that not everyone wants to be kind. Some people even see it as a weakness.

In business I have witnessed behaviours that are cruel and bullying; tactics that are used without mercy. It's quite scary to think what these people teach their children at home. Children who learn respect and empathy, and turn those principles into words and acts of kindness, can have a huge impact. They make their home and schools better places. Studies show that kind children are less likely to bully or be violent.

The benefits of kindness are huge. When you treat others with kindness, you will feel great. Just think about the last time you did something nice for someone else. How did you feel? I know that every time I do something kind –even if it's the smallest thing – I feel good. Being kind to others is also a way of being kind to yourself as we have already established.

Being kind is a way you can spread goodness in the world, a small way to make the world a better place. Whether or not you believe in karma, you must realize that when you do good things, good things happen to you. I know from personal experience that this is true. When I treat others with kindness, I find that kindness is returned to me in some form. Putting kindness into the world helps to bring a whole lot of it back to you. Acts of kindness are one of the greatest ways to inspire others. When I see someone do something out of kindness, I feel incredibly inspired and it makes me want to do something kind. When you commit a kind act, those around you will take note and your kindness can have a ripple effect.

Kindness is something we can all engage in. Kindness is a choice. You can choose it in every single situation. Whilst I know this isn't always easy, it's always possible. You may not fully realize it, but every single moment of your life, you have the choice to act in kindness.

How to cultivate kindness

The first step to kindness is being kind to yourself. You will find being kind to others very challenging if you are not very happy yourself. Happiness is a sort of kindness because, if you feel good, you will lead by example and help others to feel happy too. In the same way we can catch people's negative attitude germs, happiness is contagious. Try smiling at someone. It's very rare that we don't get rewarded with a smile back and a smile can open so many doors.

Loving kindness is very ancient, very simple, very direct and very effective. The heart of the practice for cultivating this sort of kindness is by generating four positive wishes for all beings: to be safe, to be happy, to be healthy and to be at ease.

This includes everyone we care for, those we don't care for, and those we don't care about. Naturally, it's easier to generate these positive wishes for our family and friends. It is challenging to generate that kind of attitude toward people we are indifferent to, and it is very challenging indeed to generate it toward people we don't like as I have already addressed.

To prepare the ground for practising loving kindness it can be helpful to consider that the way in which we categorize other people changes over time, sometimes very quickly, sometimes more slowly. Whatever we experience in life is subject to impermanence.

For example, a stranger we meet at a party may become our lover and, later on, can become our life partner and then in some cases an ex-partner! We have gone through all three categories with one person. Also we can recognize that the way we look at people is very much related to causes and conditions and is not absolute. If we are having a bad day it is much easier to get irritated with somebody, maybe even somebody we fundamentally like. On a beautiful sunny day, sometimes everybody looks great and we are in love with everything and feeling happy!

So causes and conditions set the stage for our attitudes toward the world; and we can, and do, affect those causes and conditions. It is practical to train our minds further so that we are not governed by our negative habitual patterns.

Finally, it is worth noting and tuning into our most fundamental nature. What are we like when we are open, clear and fully present? What is our true nature? Do we really actually wish others to suffer? Do we really wish to create the causes and conditions for our own suffering? What is wrong with cultivating open-hearted and positive wishes for ourselves and others?

So practising loving kindness is very simple. Just take a comfortable seat in a quiet place and close your eyes. First, think of somebody you love. Send them the three wishes. You can either repeat each for a time with that person in mind or just think about how those wishes might manifest and affect their situation. The tough part is to send the loving kindness to those people perhaps you don't feel so positive about. However, the process of this will not only empower you and help you to overcome any resentment or bad feeling that you have, it will strengthen your ability to cultivate genuine kindness.

Cultivating kindness: top tips

✓ Understand the difference between empathy, compassion and kindness
✓ Develop the ability to put yourself in someone else's shoes
✓ Explore the world from another person's perspective
✓ Listen to what people around you have to say
✓ Genuinely care about other people's feelings
✓ See beyond other people's negativity and feel compassion
✓ Understand the benefits of kindness for yourself and others
✓ Choose an attitude that drives kind behaviours
✓ Develop the skill of loving and unconditional kindness
✓ Review your behaviour every day and do the best you can

We make a living by what we get. We make a life by what we give.

Winston Churchill

12

MAKING A
DIFFERENCE

You're the only one who can make the difference.
Whatever your dream is, go for it.

Earvin Magic Johnson

One day a man was walking along the beach when he noticed a small boy picking something up and gently throwing it into the ocean. Approaching the boy, he asked, 'What are you doing?'

The little boy, who was called Tom, replied, 'I am saving all the starfish that have been stranded on the beach. The surf is up and the tide is going out and if I don't throw them back, they will die'.

The man looked around and noticed that there were miles and miles of beach and literally thousands of starfish.

He looked at the beach again and then at Tom and said, 'Well, you won't make much of a difference, will you?'

After listening politely, Tom bent down, picked up another starfish, and threw it back into the sea. Then, looking up, Tom smiled and said to the man, 'I made a difference for that one'.

****

I love this story and like so many of the stories in this book it illustrates a very valid point. This, however, is my favourite story simply because it highlights the ability that we all possess, it demonstrates that we all have a value and, with positive intention, we can all make a difference.

We can all have a purpose if we choose to. The key to a happy life is about discovering our purpose. Life then becomes so much more meaningful. When you can clearly define your purpose it will help you to shape your existence and help others around you. A positive purpose has to be the ultimate feel-good factor. It is the key that ignites you to feel more motivated and delighted about your life.

When you wake up every morning knowing that you can add value to the world around you, this will give you the life force and energy that sometimes may seem lacking. If you haven't defined your purpose yet then you have the opportunity right here, right now, to embark on an exciting voyage of discovery.

MEANING AND PURPOSE

When my friend Melanie's son, Matthew, was little he used to ask people, 'What are you for?' What a great question! I wonder how often we stop and ask ourselves the same question.

According to some philosophies our purpose is the central key to living a positive human life. Others believe that our purpose is not fixed and, instead, we can freely choose what we want it to be. It is, indeed, a deeply philosophical debate.

For some people, a purpose in life is an essential and fundamental aim; for other people, fulfilment and purpose is halted by fear of failure or lack of motivation or just a blind desire to want to pleasure seek for themselves only.

It would appear, however, that people who have meaning and purpose in their lives are happier, feel more in control and get more out of everything they do. They also experience less stress, less anxiety and are less prone to experiencing prolonged bouts of depression.

Something that we all need to do, rather than racing around like headless chickens wondering what it's all about, is to stop and explore our purpose.

Scientific studies of people who believe that their lives have meaning show a more positive evidence of general well-being. Martin Seligman (founder of positive psychology) describes meaning as a vital component of happiness. Having meaning in our lives is about being part of something that we really believe in that is bigger than ourselves.

It helps us to answer the burning questions: 'Why are we here?', and 'What's it all about anyway?' Often it's something that can't be distilled into one definitive answer, and goes far beyond our day-to-day activity. It guides us in how we choose to live our lives and what we strive for. It provides a framework and measurement for the goals that we set ourselves. It can help us to make sense of what happens to us. It can provide a source of comfort and strength in challenging and difficult periods of our lives. Most of all, it helps us feel that we are not alone because we are part of something much bigger.

Personally, I like the concept that we are all connected, and that if we hurt others we will only end up hurting ourselves. So we have a purpose to be kind and considerate in our behaviour towards others. By taking more personal responsibility for the consequences of our actions, our purpose becomes more honourable. If we approach every life situation with positive and kind intentions, then we will be making our own great individual contribution to creating a better world.

FINDING YOUR PURPOSE

Religion is essentially a collection of cultural and belief systems that relates humanity to spirituality and, sometimes, to a moral value which can provide meaning for many people. Research suggests that people with a faith tend to have higher average levels of happiness and well-being than people with no religious beliefs.

Religion and spirituality are not the only sources of meaning, however. For many of us, our relationships with others can provide a key source of meaning in our lives. Family, friends and the wider community can create a sense of connectivity that also provides meaning and purpose.

For some people, finding meaning comes through experiences, often difficult ones. Other people find their meaning through deep reflection, others from loving and being loved, and others just from the way they choose to approach other people and the world around. We can each find our own way – but it's good to remember the importance of meaning when making the big choices about our families, jobs, lifestyles and priorities

Some people see their meaning as finding their 'calling'. What is certain is that 'meaning' is something very personal. No one else can tell us what gives meaning to our lives and, if we rely on others rather than taking personal responsibility, we leave ourselves vulnerable. We have to discover different ways of finding meaning. We need to explore, identify and pursue our own purpose with a positive intention of making the world a better place.

GIVING

As we have already established in Chapter 11, kindness is the golden rule and the key to finding happiness as well as helping others to feel happy. Many people believe that they don't have what it takes to make a difference to the world. They believe only people like Gandhi, Mother Theresa or Albert Einstein are capable of making a difference.

The truth is that every person has the ability to contribute and make a difference to the world in their own unique way. Like the little boy in the starfish story, it need not be anything out of the world. It just needs to be something you do with the intention of doing something good.

So, if you want to feel good, do some good for other people. It may be small, unplanned acts or regular volunteering, which is a powerful way to boost our own happiness as well of those around us. The people you help may be strangers, family, friends, colleagues or neighbours. Giving to others can be as simple as a single kind word, a smile or a thoughtful gesture.

Scientific studies show that helping others boosts happiness. It increases life satisfaction, provides a sense of meaning, increases feelings of competence, improves our mood and reduces stress. It can help to take our minds off our own troubles too.

There are some strong connections between happiness and helping others. Firstly, happiness helps helping. Happy people are more likely to be interested in or be inclined towards helping others. They are more likely to have recently performed acts of kindness or spent a greater percentage of their time or money helping others

It has been assumed for a long time that giving also leads to greater happiness and this has only recently started to be scientifically proven. It makes sense that helping others contributes to our own happiness. Scientists are reconsidering the idea of the 'selfish gene' and are exploring the evolution of altruism, cooperation, compassion and kindness.

Giving isn't just about money, as some people may believe, so you don't need to wait until you win the lottery! Giving to others can be as simple as a few kind words and compliments, a smile or a thoughtful gesture. It can include giving time, care, skills, thought or attention. Sometimes these can mean more than any financial gestures. Giving also connects us to others, creating stronger communities and helping to build a happier society for everyone.

Human beings are highly social creatures and have evolved as a species living with others. If people are altruistic, they are more likely to be liked and, in turn, build better social connections and stronger, more supportive social networks, which leads to increased feelings of happiness and well-being.

It used to be thought that human beings only did things when they got something in return. How, then, could we explain people who performed kind acts or donated money anonymously? Studies of the brain now show that when we give money to good causes, the same parts of the brain light up as if we were receiving money ourselves or responding to other pleasurable things like good food, money or sex. Giving to others activates the reward centres of our brains, which make us feel good and so encourages us to do more of the same. Giving money to a good cause literally feels as good as receiving it, especially if the donations are voluntary.

Giving help has a stronger association with mental health than receiving help. Studies have shown that volunteers have fewer symptoms of depression and anxiety and they feel more hopeful. It is also related to feeling good about ourselves. It can also serve to distract people from dwelling on their own problems and to be grateful for what they have.

HOW TO MAKE A DIFFERENCE

There are so many ways that you can make a difference no matter how big or small. You too can save a starfish in so many ways.

A while ago I was doing some work in Ethiopia. On my way to work each morning in the capital of Addis Ababa, I passed a crippled man sitting in the street who each day would smile and say hello. I stopped one morning to see what he was making and noticed that he had a small box with a few plastic pens. They looked rather old and worn. He was however transforming them by very slowly and cleverly weaving the colours of the Ethiopian flag in fine thread in yellow, red and green. I complimented him on his workmanship and saw the pride in his eyes.

Each day I noticed that just a few more pens piled up in his box and I asked him how long it took to do each one. With lots of gestures I learned that he managed to do about six in a day. As I looked at his gnarled and crippled hands I realised that each one took a great deal of effort.

On my last day there I decided to buy some of the pens for my friends and family. As I walked towards him he smiled and handed me a pen and as I dipped into my pocket to pay, he shook his head and insisted I took the pen. It was a gift. This gesture touched me to the core. The fact that he could give so generously when he had so little made my heart sing.

I then insisted on buying all the pens he had, because I was able to. At this point, I realised he had given me that pen because he was able to. So the fact is we can all give. We can all share.

James Joyce, who wrote *Ulysses*, believed that we should 'Save a third, spend a third and give a third away'. I am passionate about charity, and believe that we all need to do our bit, but it is not all about money. That is helpful and all charities need it. However, time, support and contribution is hugely important.

It strikes me that the more people fill their life with materialism and toys and gadgets and designer stuff, the less time they have to think about giving. Or they believe that a big donation will assuage their conscience. Sadly, we seem to have cultivated in the Western world a 'me, me' mentality. Surely, if we spent a bit more time focusing on others, we would spend a bit less time focusing on our own issues when self-indulgence doesn't help and is counterproductive.

So start doing something positive. As Mother Theresa put it 'We cannot do great things on this Earth, only small things with great love'.

Here are a few ways that you can make a difference.

Lead the way

A good example has twice the value of good advice. When we endeavour to do things to make a difference, we should also seek to influence others to start doing things that make a difference too. The best way to convince other people is to lead by example. Start doing whatever is within your ability today. Start showing more consideration for the people you live with, work with and come into contact with each day. Every effort counts, no matter how small and insignificant it may seem. Just do something, and do something good.

Respect and value others

I mentioned in Chapter Eight the manager who left an appraisal midway through because their mobile phone went off and, essentially, something better or more important came along. It seems that this kind of mentality is flourishing. We live in a world where everything is disposable, it can all be replaced, even relationships. Or at least that seems to be the perception.

How often do you see people on their mobile phones not even making eye contact, let alone engaging, with someone they may be doing a transaction with? Giving people your full attention is not only kind, it shows respect and good manners. Next time you engage with someone, look them in the eye, smile and say thank you. It's the little things that count.

Listen to other people

Listening to other people without passing judgment is one of the kindest things you can do. Some people may want to share a problem and maybe they know the answers to the problems they are facing, they just haven't realized it yet. By letting them talk it through you can help them. Sometimes they might need encouragement and help to start on this new path; sometimes they may need your practical support; and sometimes they may just want you to sit and listen.

People also want to share positive experiences. Being able to enthuse and tell someone all about a new relationship, a holiday or a successful work achievement can make the experience all the more exciting. Listen and live it with them because it will make them happy.

Stick up for other people

I am sure that you have witnessed someone getting treated unfairly. It happens both professionally and socially, sometimes individuals who deserve recognition do not get it. Perhaps they are scared of confrontation and find it hard to stand up for themselves. By taking up the fight and making sure others get what they deserve, you will make a lasting impact on their lives. They, in turn, will get the justice they merit and feel better. Be careful that you get all the information right though before you go jumping in feet first!

Support charity

There are various charities that I actively support and we all make choices as to which ones we want to devote our time and money to. There are so many different ways that you can do your bit. Whatever motivates and inspires you, it's more than likely that the charity you choose to support will be inspired by an experience in your life, and something you feel passionate about.

Years ago, when I lived in London, I was walking along Oxford Street in subzero temperatures and, lying on the ground, was a man shivering with a filthy blanket wrapped tightly around him. I decided that I would go and buy him a large cup of hot tea which I put down next to him. As I walked away, I noticed two very well presented strangers pointing at the man and laughing at him. I remember this really upset me and, as I walked home, angry and frustrated, I decided I wanted to channel my emotional energy into something constructive.

On the back of that experience I set up a charity support group for Barnados, which funded a project to support keeping young children off the streets in Camden. Actively fund raising for the project for two years was an eye opener. I learnt a lot about generosity and kindness and how amazingly supportive people can be. If people couldn't give money, they gave time and support. I also learnt how challenging it can be for many organizations that are trying to raise money and cannot rally the support they need.

Charity shops are a great way to do your bit. We all have things, I am sure, that we keep in cupboards because we think we may need them one day. However, how much stuff do we really need? I cringe when I hear celebrities boasting that they have hundreds of pairs of shoes sitting in their cupboards. When we look at how many spare of everything we have, it can seem quite greedy. This weekend why not declutter your life, get a big bag and go and share all the extra things you really don't need and will possibly never use again with your local charity shop?

When it comes to charity if everyone just does a little it can make a giant difference.

Random acts of kindness

There are so many that you can do. It's the little things that can make another person's day, like helping someone with a heavy case or a pram, holding open a door, picking up some litter. It really doesn't need to be huge. Having the courage to compliment someone if they look nice can make someone glow all day. You have most likely been on the receiving end of some kind act, so I am sure you know how good it makes you feel. There is also a website in my top ten happy website lists at the back the book that is about random acts of kindness. This will give you some inspiration.

I read somewhere about a woman who always carried a spare umbrella with her when it rained, so that if ever someone had been caught out she was on offer to lend a hand. I found this really touching. The pre thought is great and a really good way to condition our minds to be kind. Proactively, thinking of ways to help out. I like that.

There are so many heartwarming stories of kindness, small thoughtful actions that everyone has the ability to do. Wherever you are, and whatever you are doing, there will be opportunities. At home it could be making sure that you don't make your loved ones feel taken for granted: a little gift under a pillow, a surprise meal, or doing the washing up when it's not your turn!

At work it could be just ensuring that you make somewhere tidy before someone else needs to work there, or buying someone a box of chocolates or a bottle of wine to say thanks for helping you on a work project. It's worth making a conscious effort to recognize when someone has done something well, to say thank you and just let them know that you appreciate them.

Anywhere you find yourself, life is bound to present you with opportunities. It pays to be on the lookout. Get into the habit of doing something every day that makes you proud because someone else has directly benefitted from it.

Be happy

Happiness and love are the two greatest gifts you can give to the world. Too often, we're too absorbed in own little bubble and we forget there are people in this world who we can make a little happier and who we can make feel a little more loved.

Make a difference right now to yourself and the world around you and be happy.

Make a difference: top tips

✓ Identify your purpose and meaning in life
✓ Make a decision to seek out opportunities to be kind
✓ Practise kindness on a daily basis
✓ Lead the way and set positive examples
✓ Respect and value other people
✓ Listen to what other people have to say
✓ Stick up for other people when they are treated unfairly
✓ Support a charity or volunteer for a community project
✓ Demonstrate random acts of kindness
✓ Make a difference right now – be happy

Nobody can do everything, but everyone can do something

Author unknown

HAPPY RESOURCES

TOP TEN – HAPPY WEBSITES

There are more and more websites now emerging which focus on the positive things in life. Here are my top ten favourites that offer some great advice.

1. Action for Happiness

www.actionforhappiness.org

Action for Happiness is a movement for positive social change. It aims to bring together people from all walks of life who want to play a part in creating a happier society for everyone. I strongly recommend that you register and join the movement. It will positively change your life as well as benefitting others at the same time!

2. Random Acts of Kindness

www.randomactsofkindness.org

The Random Acts of Kindness Foundation is an internationally recognized non-profit organization founded upon the powerful belief in kindness and dedicated to providing resources and tools that encourage acts of kindness.

3. Happy News

www.happynews.com

This website believes virtue, goodwill and heroism are hot news. That's why the site shows up-to-the-minute news, geared to lift spirits and inspire lives. Add in a diverse team of Citizen Journalists reporting positive stories from around the world, and you've got one happy place for news.

4. Happy Planet Index

www.happyplanetindex.org

A site that measures the well-being of people in the nations of the world while taking into account their environmental impact. It makes very interesting reading.

5. Authentic Happiness

www.authentichappiness.sas.upenn.edu

Authentic Happiness is the homepage of Dr. Martin Seligman, Director of the Positive Psychology Center at the University of Pennsylvania and founder of positive psychology, a branch of psychology which focuses on the empirical study of such things as positive emotions, strengths-based character, and healthy institutions.

6. Happy Simple Living

www.happysimpleliving.com

A very positive site which explores many of subjects: simplicity, home, family, good food, personal finance and sustainable living.

7. The Way to Happiness

www.thewaytohappiness.org

The first moral code based wholly on common sense, originally published in 1981, its purpose is to help arrest the current moral decline in society and restore integrity and trust to man. *The Way to Happiness* further holds a Guinness Record as the single most translated site.

8. Laugh Alive

www.laughtergym.com

This is a fabulous website full of really interesting information about laughter. Laughter therapy is the latest stress-busting, health-enhancing trend to take the wellbeing world by storm. According to new research we've never needed it more and many of us fail to enjoy a proper belly laugh even just once a day and the amount we laugh on a daily basis is a staggering three times lower than it was in the 1950s.

9. World Kindness

www.worldkindness.org.sg

The idea behind the World Kindness Movement (WKM) crystallised at a conference in Tokyo in 1997 when the Small Kindness Movement of Japan brought together like-minded kindness movements from around the world. The mission of the WKM is to inspire individuals towards greater kindness and to connect nations to create a kinder world.

10. My Website

www.liggywebb.com

I had to mention this one because there is a whole range of free downloadable materials that are all geared to help promote health and happiness. Please do visit and take advantage of what is on offer.

TOP TEN – HAPPY FILMS

I love watching really uplifting and positive films and here is my top ten favourites which I highly recommend watching to lift your spirits and make you feel good.

1. It's a Wonderful Life (1946) – Prescribed by psychiatrists as a remedy for their patient's depression, "It's A Wonderful Life" is Hollywood's answer for increasing those serotonin levels. It remains a firm favourite amongst audiences for its life-affirming story and James Stewart's wonderful performance.

2. The Shawshank Redemption (1994) – Frank Darabont's prison drama "The Shawshank Redemption" is one of the best movies ever made. This film epitomizes the power of optimism and has some wonderfully inspiring moments that will provide you with the ultimate feel good factor!

3. Little Miss Sunshine (2006) – Road movies seem to be a great starting point for happy films. It is after all a journey that the audience and the characters take, discovering humanity and their own humanness along the way. "Little Miss Sunshine" is a vibrant, hopeful, and funny film with some wonderful characters and performances.

4. Amelie (2001) – "Amelie" is a sugar-coated, rose-tinted story of self-discovery set against the backdrop of a picture-perfect Paris. The city is painted in vibrant hues to encapsulate the romanticism of the place everyone goes to in order to fall in love, or so the film would have you believe.

5. Forrest Gump (1994) – Life is like a box of chocolates! Robert Zemeckis' film is both sentimental and epic in scope. With a great performance from Tom Hanks and a wonderfully orchestrated whistle-stop tour of American history it will soar your spirit and I think . . .

6. Duck Soup (1933) – On its release in 1933 "Duck Soup" wasn't considered as anything special. How opinion has changed. Now it is generally considered a masterpiece and arguably the finest film made by the Marx Brothers.

7. Finding Nemo (2003) – Pixar's best film is about a clownfish on an adventure across the ocean to find his son. It's a heart-warming tale of familial loyalty and friendship, set against the backdrop of Pixar's scintillating computer generated ocean.

8. Life Is Beautiful (1997) Roberto Benigni who made this wonderful tale that celebrates the human spirit. It will pull at your heartstrings but "Life Is Beautiful" is all about the vitality of life in the midst of the destructiveness of war. Roger Ebert said it perfectly; ""Life Is Beautiful" is not about Nazis and Fascists, but about the human spirit.'

9. E.T – The Extra-Terrestrial (1982) – Two lost and innocent children – one human, one alien – find friendship and adventure in a Californian suburb. The film might be otherworldly but its message is universally appealing. By the end you'll be weeping with happy tears and going right back to the start for another magical journey.

10. Mary Poppins (1964). This musical film is my favourite film of all time. Starring Julie Andrews and Dick Van Dyke, produced by Walt Disney, and based on the Mary Poppins books series by P. L. Travers. Julie Andrews epitomizes positivity throughout and she won the Academy Award for Best Actress for her performance as Mary Poppins. It really is a joyful experience.

TOP TEN – HAPPY SONGS

Listening to music has scientifically been proven to cause the brain to release dopamine which is a feel good chemical. So if you want to get a happy high I thoroughly recommend these uplifting tracks:

1. Louis Armstrong – What A Wonderful World

2. M People – Proud

3. Jackson 5 – Blame It On The Boogie

4. Captain Sensible – Happy Talk

5. The Beloved – Sweet Harmony

6. Eliza Doolittle – Pack it up

7. The Carpenters – Top Of The World

8. Michael Jackson – Man In The Mirror

9. Aretha Franklin – Oh Happy Day

10. ABBA – Dancing Queen

. . . AND TEN HAPPY CLASSICAL MUSIC PIECES

Both my father and my brother and my nephew play the piano beautifully and I have been fortunate enough to be surrounded by classical music all my life. These are my top ten feel good favourites.

1. Claude Debussy – Clair De Lune

2. Johann Pachelbel – Canon in D

3. Edward Elgar – Nimrod

4. Pyotr Ilyich Tchaikovsky – The Nutcracker Suite & Swan Lake

5. Edvard Grieg – 'Peer Gynt' Suite No. 1, Op. 46 – Morning

6. Johann Strauss – Blue Danube

7. Frederic Chopin – Nocturn

8. Alexander Borodin – Polovtsian Dance from "Prince Igor"

9. Gioachino Rossini – Overture from "Barber of Seville"

10. Nikolai Rimsky-Korsakov – Flight of the Bumblebee

TOP TEN – HAPPY QUOTES

Finally, as you can tell from reading this book, I love quotes. All my life certain quotes have resonated so strongly and my home is literally decorated with words of wisdom that reinforce the hope and optimism that keeps us going and keeps us strong .Here is a top ten of my favourites that I haven't managed to weave into the book.

1. Leo. F. Buscaglia

Happiness is having a sense of self – not a feeling of being perfect but of being good enough and knowing that you are in the process of growth, of being, of achieving levels of joy. It's a wonderful contentment and acceptance of who and what you are and a knowledge that the world and the life are full of wondrous adventures and possibilities, and you are part of the centre. It's an awareness that no matter what happens you will somehow be able to deal with it, knowing that everything does pass and even your deepest despair will vanish.

2. William Shakespeare

This above all, to thine own self be true.

3. Oscar Wilde

Some cause happiness wherever they go; others, whenever they go.

4. Ralph Waldo Emerson 1803–1882

To laugh often and much;
To win the respect of intelligent people and the affection of children;
To earn the appreciation of honest critics and endure the betrayal of false friends;

To appreciate beauty, to find the best in others;
To leave the world a bit better, whether by a healthy child, a garden
patch, or a redeemed social condition;
To know even one life has breathed easier because you have lived.
This is to have succeeded.

5. Helen Keller

Although the world is full of suffering . . . it is also full of overcoming it.

6. Joseph Campbell

It's only by going down into the abyss
that we recover the treasures of life.
Where you stumble
there lies your treasure.
The very cave you are afraid to enter
turns out to be the source of
what you were looking for.

7. Aristotle

Happiness is the meaning and the purpose of life, the whole aim and
end of human existence

8. Harriet Meyerson

Happiness comes only from appreciating what you have right now.
You can even be happy by appreciating your troubles because they
are helping to build your character.

9. Mark Twain

Whoever is happy will make others happy, too.

10. Buddha

You, yourself, as much as anybody in the entire universe, deserve your love and affection.

INDEX